"Leroy Barber has been on the frontlines of the strugg
now. In his new book *Embrace*, he makes the case for
tionships, especially with people who are unlike us,
kingdom here on earth and repairing the breaches in
that talk isn't enough—that we need to repair the breac... ...have caused and allowed in both our relationships and our systems. Leroy Barber is making a powerful case today for why leaders of color need our strongest affirmation and support, especially in faith-based and other critical nonprofit organizations, if we are to move forward."

Jim Wallis, president, Sojourners, editor in chief, *Sojourners*, *New York Times*–bestselling author of *America's Original Sin*

"A powerful book for these times. The weave of the biblical story, current times, and the personal journey of Leroy Barber bring the reader to more fully understand, embrace, and find the courage to live out radical shalom. I believe this book should be read by every person who is a Christ follower. Could it be the groundbreaker for the racial healing that is so desperately needed and that our Lord desires to accomplish? An unequivocal yes!"

Jo Anne Lyon, general superintendent, The Wesleyan Church

"Troubled times require God's people to rise up and embody God's shalom. Leroy Barber fully understands the world we live in. His life and ministry reveal a deep concern for our divided and broken world. He not only writes about shalom relationships but also demonstrates them in his own life and ministry. This book will lead you through important but sometimes difficult concepts and issues that can strengthen the church and direct you toward an embodied life of godly relationships that we will do well to emulate."

Soong-Chan Rah, Milton B. Engebretson Professor of Church Growth and Evangelism, North Park Theological Seminary, author of *Prophetic Lament*

"With powerful stories and fresh insight, Leroy challenges us to fall in love with hard places and see the image of God in hard people. We are reminded that the hard places are exactly where we need to be. *Embrace* illustrates the many ways God uses difficult situations in life to help us love more deeply and bring us closer to one another and God."

Shawn Casselberry, executive director, Mission Year

"Leroy Barber offers a simple yet deeply profound invitation to return to a foundation of relationship. *Embrace* is very timely with helpful insights for today's increasingly divided world. Barber challenges us to look and find the unexamined prejudices that lead us to further alienation from those God brings into our lives. A great book for those longing for depth and true transformation in their relationships."

Nikki Toyama-Szeto, director, IJM Institute for Biblical Justice, author of *God of Justice*

"*Embrace* is an important book for this kairos moment in history. Many of us in the church long for true racial reconciliation. We want to be peacemakers in this broken and angry world. However, we often lack concrete, down-to-earth, timely, and biblically based tools for building real relationships across the lines. Rev. Barber has given us a wealth of wisdom for how to make these dreams real. He helps us understand and, yes, embrace one another."

Alexia Salvatierra, pastor, founder, The Faith-Rooted Organizing UnNetwork, coauthor of *Faith-Rooted Organizing*

"In *Embrace* Leroy Barber shows us that loving our neighbor includes knowing and relating to one another. With years of wisdom and experience, Leroy beautifully and patiently shows us how we can become the beloved community we were created to be. If you're looking for a practical and hopeful book to help you navigate some of the deep divides that plague our culture, look no further. This book is insightful, encouraging, and a delight to read!"

Ken Wytsma, president, Kilns College, author of *Pursuing Justice* and *Create vs. Copy*

"*Embrace* is a practical road map for radically living into God's shalom in a divided world. With over thirty years of experience in building community both domestically and internationally, there is no better person than Leroy Barber to show us the power of living into God's embrace of diversity."

Romal Tune, senior advisor to the president, The Mission Society for Diversity and Inclusion Initiatives, CEO, Clerestory: Ministry and Leadership in a New Light

"In the Bible, righteousness is all about relationships. To be righteous means to be rightly related with all those elements that make up human life. And God knows we can all do with some help in this regard. My dear friend Leroy is a man who knows how to enhance his world through loving relationships. In this book he helps us be more righteous in very practical, joy-filled, and life-giving ways."

Debra Hirsch, author of *Redeeming Sex* and *Untamed*

"We live in an era of polarization, where everyone is encouraged to choose a label, to associate only with others who carry the same label, and to view all others as the enemy. It is to this deeply divided world that Leroy Barber's *Embrace* speaks. Deftly weaving reflections on Scripture with his long history of crossing racial, ethnic, and economic barriers, Leroy reminds us that Christian tradition calls us to be one family with those we see as radically different from ourselves. He provides concrete strategies for living in community in the midst of division and turmoil. Whether you are crossing boundaries for the first time or a seasoned practitioner of reconciliation, *Embrace* is a challenge and an inspiration to live into the Christian call to reconciliation."

Chanequa Walker-Barnes, author of *Too Heavy a Yoke*

"*Embrace* brings us back to what's most fundamental about our humanity: relationships. With a perfect blend of pastoral compassion and prophetic conviction, Leroy guides us down the often messy path of reconciliation while remaining firmly centered in the heart of Christ and renouncing a posture and politics of fear."

Rachel Goble, president, The SOLD Project

Embrace

GOD'S RADICAL SHALOM FOR A DIVIDED WORLD

LEROY BARBER

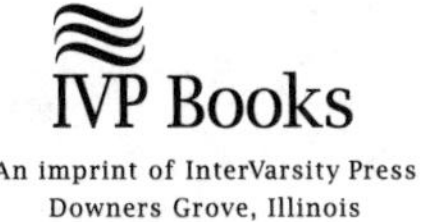

An imprint of InterVarsity Press
Downers Grove, Illinois

InterVarsity Press
P.O. Box 1400, Downers Grove, IL 60515-1426
ivpress.com
email@ivpress.com

InterVarsity Press® is the book-publishing division of InterVarsity Christian Fellowship/USA®, a movement of students and faculty active on campus at hundreds of universities, colleges, and schools of nursing in the United States of America, and a member movement of the International Fellowship of Evangelical Students. For information about local and regional activities, visit intervarsity.org.

While any stories in this book are true, some names and identifying information may have been changed to protect the privacy of individuals.

Cover design: Cindy Kiple
Interior design: Beth McGill

ISBN 978-0-8308-4471-5 (print)
ISBN 978-0-8308-7318-0 (digital)

Printed in the United States of America ♾

As a member of the Green Press Initiative, InterVarsity Press is committed to protecting the environment and to the responsible use of natural resources. To learn more, visit greenpressinitiative.org.

Library of Congress Cataloging-in-Publication Data

A catalog record for this book is available from the Library of Congress.

P 25 24 23 22 21 20 19 18 17 16 15 14 13 12 11 10 9 8 7 6 5 4 3 2 1
Y 34 33 32 31 30 29 28 27 26 25 24 23 22 21 20 19 18 17 16

This book is dedicated to all those for whom I have the honor of being called friend, especially my wife Donna, and our five children—we have been on an incredible journey together. For all my friends, I am thankful.

CONTENTS

Introduction / 9

1 Embracing the Place / 13

2 The Ones We Avoid / 27

3 God Likes Pumpkin Pie / 41

4 Looking at Change the Right Way / 57

5 Going the Distance / 67

6 Take Me Out to the Ball Game / 84

7 Natural Justice / 100

8 Loving Even Our Enemies / 109

9 Yes, Black Lives Matter! / 121

Acknowledgments / 137

Notes / 139

INTRODUCTION

I wrote this book because we're in some trying times. We don't know each other, and it's causing us to hurt each other. It's breaking down political systems. It's allowing injustice to continue and violence to run rampant in the world. And the greatest power we have to change this—relationships—is not being used as much as it could. We need to make a push toward deepening our relationships. If we do, we'll see God's kingdom break through our chaos.

Good relationships make the world go 'round. I don't think there's anything more powerful. Donna and I had the chance to go back to Philly a few years ago to celebrate the one-hundredth anniversary of the church we grew up in together. Our friends—some who now live in different places around the country and many who still live in Philly—gathered to reflect on the past and catch up on life. We hadn't been together in many years, but when we entered the room it seemed like it had been no time at all. We connected instantly, and before we knew it, hours had gone by as we laughed together over our kids and the past and our current lives. Relationships run deep. They stay with us and shape us in ways we don't always expect.

Relationships have also been the saving grace many times in my life. It was the store owner who called my mom rather than the police when I was dumb enough to take a bag of chips. It was my best friend who helped me pass classes I should have failed. You have stories of times when friends saved you and when you saved friends from potentially horrific things in life. Relationships are a true source of grace in our lives.

Relationships can bring us complete joy. You know the time you had so much fun with friends that you talk about it for years—it makes you smile just thinking about it because it's set so deeply in that good place in your soul. It's the birth of a child, the completion of a work project with trusted colleagues, your wedding day, a vacation, an intimate relationship that resounds in your being for a lifetime . . . relationships are a source of true joy.

But relationships have also been the source of pain in our lives. The trusted relationship that's gone bad and caused us to react negatively or start destructive behaviors. The parent that leaves or abuses, the friend who betrays or the coach that acts inappropriately. These abuses of relationships send us in tailspins. Many of us will cope and recover, but some of us will not. Relationships can break us and contribute to the brokenness in this world.

Think about it right now: Did you get where you are alone, or are there relational ties to your current situation? Wherever you are, there was a relationship involved. We are not just isolated individuals—we are part of a big conglomeration of relationships. We don't accomplish things on our merit alone; we often benefit because of who we know and who we associate with. The job you have: Who recommended you? The place you live: Who told you about it? The store where you shop, the place where you get your hair cut, the new song you just listened to, the bank you use, the school you attend . . . the list of the ways we count on our friends can go on forever. We are not self-made. We are community made, each and every one of us. And when we witness some great good, there are without a doubt relational dynamics behind the scene that made the difference.

When we create opportunities for people to connect, we create opportunities for the world to become a better place. Have you ever heard someone say, *It's not personal*? (I wholeheartedly despise those words—they're usually harmful and always personal to someone.) I'm writing this book so that the *personal* drives our decisions. We must make the world more personal so that we can care for one another in ways that lift each other up and invite creativity instead of fostering distrust. Treaties and policies created in spaces of distrust either won't last or will forever be the source of more pain and continued distrust. Hatred and distrust will only breed hatred and distrust. But when people love and the personal is at the center, we create more love and deeper relationships. Love doesn't birth hatred—it provides the soil for human flourishing. And we respond to love with passion, creativity, life, hope, and justice.

On my best days I am decent pastor. My call as a pastor is most realized when I stand with and for others. I hope to inspire you not only to better love the people close to you but to take a chance on loving someone you would rather avoid. I have found the best places of learning to be in the unexpected relationships with the "other" in my life. When I have embraced the people farthest from me, it has opened a space for others and myself to grow. When we first started in ministry, we befriended a person who lived on the streets. As James started coming around, it caused others to think about how they engaged people living on the streets and opened up the option to talk with and befriend them. A space was created—the possibility of getting to know the other—because getting to know the other was modeled for them.

In this book we take a look at Jeremiah's word to the people of Israel when they were in exile—his word about the hard folks they didn't like and who had treated them poorly. We look at

God's call to love people when it's not easy. When we establish relationships in places where they're not expected, we'll see in chapter one those relationships drive change and open pathways to healing. This is a call to create good ground for justice to take root. We must continue to call out injustice and stand unapologetically against systems that dishonor people.

In chapter two, we look at the folks we would rather keep at a distance and how those initial judgments can lead to a relational breakdown or a deep friendship depending on our response. In chapter three, we examine differences as something beautiful, not as a cause for division, and how we can learn to appreciate them. Chapter four challenges our notions of change—how change can be a healthier process if welcomed—followed by chapter five and the idea of commitment to stay for the long term in our difficult relationships. Chapter six looks at traditions and how nourishing them can bring us to a powerful place with the other. Chapter seven argues that justice may play out naturally as we seek to be closer. Chapter eight is about the hard place of loving the folks who treat us wrong. Then in chapter nine we look at the current question of Black Lives Matter. I pray this journey is helpful to you and that at the end of this book the other in your life will be drawn a little closer to home.

While I trust that this entire book will be filled with hope and encouragement for you, I want to end it by grounding us in the faithfulness of God and in his promises to and for us. I'd like us all to catch a vision of what Christ had in mind when he prayed that his kingdom would come on earth and that we might find in all our brothers and sisters the unity that he shared with the Father.

1

EMBRACING THE PLACE

This is what the LORD Almighty, the God of Israel, says to all those I carried into exile from Jerusalem to Babylon: "Build houses and settle down; plant gardens and eat what they produce. Marry and have sons and daughters; find wives for your sons and give your daughters in marriage, so that they too may have sons and daughters. Increase in number there; do not decrease. Also, seek the peace and prosperity of the city to which I have carried you into exile. Pray to the LORD for it, because if it prospers, you too will prosper."

JEREMIAH 29:4-7

Babylon.

Even today, more than two thousand years after the city slid into relative insignificance, its name invokes nightmarish images. Debauchery. Self-indulgence. Abusive power. Idolatry. Confusion. Enslavement of weaker peoples and nations. Babylon was dangerous and overwhelming. The women were fast, the men slick, and the rulers were ruthless egomaniacs.

The reputation of Babylon has far outlasted its existence. Though the evidence of its might and decadence has been buried for more than two millennia, Babylon remains a synonym—*the* synonym—for ungodly depravity and corruption. If ever there was a Godforsaken place, Babylon was it, and God's people did well to stay as far away as possible.

And yet somehow Babylon was where the remnant of God's chosen people found themselves in the days of Jeremiah the prophet. I think the people of Israel may, at least in moments of honesty, have realized their own complicity in these bad circumstances—they may have understood how far they had strayed from their part of the covenant God had made with them. But I suspect that their feelings were dominated by disbelief that Babylon—this hard place in which they found themselves—was where they were meant to be. I'm sure they questioned daily whether it was in fact God's will for them to be there of all places.

And when a letter arrived from the Lord—through his prophet, Jeremiah—I'll just bet they believed it was going to say, "Don't worry; I'll have you out of there very soon. You've learned your lesson, and I'm coming right away to free you. Don't even bother unpacking your things—my plan all along has been to bring you straight back to the land of promise, your homeland, the place of my blessing and prosperity. I don't want you in Babylon any longer."

But that wasn't how the Lord's message read. Oh, it did contain a promise of eventual deliverance—but that deliverance didn't apply to the generation of people hearing it. As they heard the letter being read, they may have taken some comfort on behalf of their children and grandchildren, but for the listeners themselves, the Lord's message was clear: *You* are to put down roots in the place you now find yourselves; I have no plans to deliver *you*; my will for *your* lives is that you live in Babylon.

I imagine that the confessions and prayers for God's mind to change were heavy. The *I'm sorry* prayers, the *I will do anything you say God, just get us out of here!* prayers. You know those prayers where you bargain with God? The ones where you beg and plead for your situation to be changed? Those prayers don't always work. Most times God sets the course and we must comply.

A PHILLY KID IN THE SOUTH

Have you ever found yourself in your own personal Babylon? Have you ever landed in a place you would not have chosen—one that you were certain could not be the right fit for you, your gifts and talents, your likes and dislikes? Maybe even now you and your family are in a hard place and wondering whether the call you felt was really the Lord's.

When I was a kid, my grandfather would pile us into the van for our yearly journey from Philadelphia to Monroeville, Alabama. We would spend hours and hours on the road, stopping only at rest stops and gas stations as we journeyed south toward our family. For this Philly kid, it was somewhat bittersweet. I remember the hours squeezed into that van as some of the fondest moments of my life. But I also remember the heat of Alabama mixed with the smell of my aunt's farm (and the flies that were constantly biting) as we sat in that country place my mother and grandparents seemed to love so much. And I remember declaring that I would never live in the South: it was too slow, too hot, too backward, and the people talked funny. Somewhere hidden in the recesses of my heart was the idea that

I was better than my family in the South. I never said it, but truth be told, it was there.

I think there were also many questions in the back of my mind about the South as it pertained to race. We rarely ventured into places where white people were, even though I knew they were around. I overheard stories about how my family was treated that seemed to suggest negative things. There were no relationships between races—no common spaces and no social networks that included anyone of another race. I was very young then, but the uneasiness was real. The South's racial undertones were tucked away in my heart, but they would not be processed with anyone of another race until much later in my life.

So that is why I said that I would never live in the South. Have you ever said something like *I would never* or *over my dead body* or even just thought it? Words and attitudes like those sit there and begin to make their way to our hearts and eventually our actions toward the other. Generally this is not a good thing. Perhaps our lack of embrace started with a mini unspoken declaration in reaction to some event in our lives and later shows itself in how we dishonor people who are not like ourselves. These unspoken attitudes can make it harder for us to hear the voice of God when we are called to love and relate with folks who are different than we are accustomed to. Certain actions and ideas will seem crazy, no matter how large or small they seem. Even a simple request to go and have lunch with someone different becomes a major challenge. I can't tell you how many times suggesting the simple task of having lunch at a different table or playing basketball with a different group has been a source of tension. You would think I had asked people to give up a body part or something.

Once I asked Stephanie, who was an athlete at her school, to go over to a table of basketball players and introduce herself and let them know how much she loved b-ball. She turned beet red and began shaking her head. "They're all black," she said. I tried to convince her, but she seemed pretty fearful. A year later, I went back to speak at Stephanie's school and she walked right up to me and introduced her friend Byron, a tall African American young man. She smiled and said, "I went over to the table." Stephanie got past the fear of the other and, in doing so, she gained a friend. They didn't solve the problems of the world with one relationship, but they offer us a tad of hope. In the next racially tense situation or conversation they'll have a foundation of friendship to help solve the problem.

EXILED FROM PHILLY

Thirty years after my childhood declaration about the South, I was on a plane on my way back to Philly from a recruitment trip to Atlanta, trying to contain tears. I was attempting to think of a way to share with my wife, Donna, my church, and the head of the ministry where I worked that I believed God was calling us to Atlanta. I loved (and continue to adore) Philadelphia. I was an ambassador of the City of Brotherly Love and led hundreds of interns, students, and guests on tours around the city I cared about so deeply. And Atlanta was in the South, the place I vowed never to live. But God was about to show me who was really in charge—he was very clear that we were to live in Atlanta, and his voice only became stronger and the confirmations more numerous. We had no choice but to move to Atlanta. Babylon it would be: the place that had been good for a visit but not for home, and the place I secretly despised. An exile of sorts was before me, and like the ancient Israelites, I hoped it would be for a short time. I didn't see Atlanta as a long-term thing. "We can stay about five years at the most," I declared to Donna and anyone else in Philly who would ask. "We will be back."

Fast forward sixteen years of life in Atlanta. I was on the board of Word Made Flesh, and we were in the midst of some transition. The home offices were about to be relocated to Portland, Oregon. I had zero problems with the relocation of Word Made Flesh to Oregon. I figured, "If white folks want to live in white-land, no problem!" Little did I know that a few months later I would become the executive director and be moving my family to one of the whitest states in the Union. Yet another place I would never have considered living. It's West Coast *and* white—I'm East Coast all the way and black, and after sixteen years I had come to *love* Atlanta! We raised our kids there, bought a home there, settled into ministry and life there. Portland represented for me *Babylon the Sequel.*

In weighing the move to Portland I was reminded of how faithful God had been in our transition to Atlanta. I remembered the amazing ways God had provided community for us in what was once a strange place, and I was convicted for even beginning to doubt him. Doubt is natural, but what God had done for our family was undeniable. So maybe my doubt was not about provision at all. Was my heart hard toward this place where whiteness was so celebrated? Yeah, it sure was. But I found myself back in the place where I had to recognize who was calling the shots. When God is the One who calls us to a place, then God will make a space for us there. I knew that was true and I had to accept it.

We live in Portland. In fact, we made it our home even after I transitioned out of the organization that brought us here. After living in a personal Babylon twice, I'm convinced that Babylon is where God works on us best. Too many times our "mission" is about us and keeping comfortable in our biases. But sometimes it's only in Babylon that we listen.

My biases were what caused the most angst in me when I heard the words *Atlanta* or *Portland*. *Atlanta* meant "backward," and I couldn't see myself in that space. Even though I had never lived in Atlanta or spent much time there, I had a fully formed opinion of it. That's how we usually address the other in our lives and that's what makes it easy for us to dehumanize people. When we have opinions about a group of people without having a personal relationship with them, we are on the path to dehumanizing them. If you add influence to the equation, you create the possibility for mass dehumanization—attitudes of a large group of people toward another large group of people. Add dynamics of power, and you can create systems that harm the other.

Using this kind of power and influence with our biases would be like me making Atlanta to be like Philadelphia just because I thought Philly was a better place. That would have been horrible for Atlanta. Instead I moved into Atlanta and learned the culture, and they learned me, and together we created some beautiful things. Atlanta Youth Academy is one of those things. It's a school in the city created so that families struggling economically can have access to quality Christian education. Atlanta Youth Academy is a combination of the Barber family's Philly attitude and Larry Teem's southern ways (more about Larry later in this chapter). The combination wasn't always pretty—but God was in it. Another one of those beautiful things was Community Fellowships, a combination of a church, youth development program, and community of friends across race and culture that paved the way for many wonderful things to happen in Atlanta. Community Fellowships was the catalyst for Mission Year in Atlanta and the incubator for many leaders of all ages and races. It was fun in the streets of East Lake and south Atlanta. Atlanta was nothing like Philly, but it had its own joys. The messiness of reaching across boundaries to the other was the catalyst for joy. When we embrace hard places and hard people in our lives, we can create amazing things together—risks worth taking.

HARD PLACES, HARD PEOPLE

Some people and places are just plain hard—there's no question about it. There are some situations and combinations of people and place that everyone—those on the outside *and* those on the inside—would agree are hard. But in many situations with hard places and hard people, what makes them hard is that they are *different* from what we're used to. We perceive them as hard not because they are inherently so but because they make us uncomfortable. They're hard because we don't understand the way they talk, look, or behave. They're hard because we can't see that we have much, if anything, in common with them—worldview, values, likes, and dislikes.

But those people might have a completely different perspective. The place where they live—the place we find to be so hard—might be everything they want in a city. And they might be so comfortable with their own neighbors—the people we find so hard—that they can't imagine having to move away and find community elsewhere. Even Babylon may have been like this—I believe that many Babylonians loved their city, their neighborhood, and the families that lived nearby.

Throughout this book, we'll use the account of God's people in Babylon and other biblical examples as starting points for a conversation about how God might intend for us to live in harmony and shalom in the toughest situations we encounter. You've either been or now find yourself in a hard place and dealing with hard people, or maybe those trials are still ahead of you. Either way, we all find ourselves in a world of broken relationships (as the news daily reminds us) and it is followers of Christ—his appointed ministers of reconciliation (2 Cor 5:18-20)—who have the required tools, motivation, and Spirit of love that can accomplish the redemption of the hard things around us today.

THE CALL TO EMBRACE

The exiles of Jeremiah's day had no choice in the matter of their relocation. They were forcefully taken to Babylon—ripped from their homes and made to march away from the lands they knew and loved. But what about the person (the son or daughter of God) who is not yet in the hard place because he or she has refused God's clear call to go there? This was the case with Jonah.

"The word of the Lord came to Jonah son of Amittai: 'Go to the great city of Nineveh and preach against it, because its wickedness has come up before me.' But Jonah ran away from the Lord and headed for Tarshish" (Jon 1:1-3). Jonah knew where God wanted him to be, but he chose to head in the opposite direction. God's call couldn't have been any clearer. Jonah had no doubts about where he was supposed to be, but he saw Nineveh as a hard place.

He had good reason to do so. Nineveh was the last capital of the great Assyrian empire and a perennial foe of Jonah's people, the Israelites. Like Babylon—Jonah's story probably takes place about two hundred years prior to the exile in Babylon—Nineveh was idolatrous and violent, conquering the surrounding lands and taking their peoples into slavery. Jonah, as I said, had good reasons to wish to be elsewhere.

As Jonah's story unfolds, the Lord manipulates creation itself—storms at sea and a great fish (or whale)—to compel Jonah to reach Nineveh. Once there, Jonah carries out God's instructions, warning the Ninevites of their need to change their ways and their hearts. And they do. The Ninevites change. The point of the account is that, as hard and evil as Nineveh seemed to be, it was not outside the scope of God's mercy, forgiveness, and redemption. There is not and never has been such a thing as a "Godforsaken" place. In contemporary terms, the book of Jonah teaches us that there is no city, no barrio, no precinct or neighborhood, no turf that is outside of God's great plan of redemption. And just as God used Jonah, an outsider, to teach the people of Nineveh about God's great love and forgiveness, Christ calls his followers today to go into "all Judea and Samaria, and to the ends of the earth" (Acts 1:8)—which includes a whole lot of what we may consider hard people and hard places—to share the good news of the kingdom.

Let me say this as clearly as I can: the message of the book of Jonah is that God's love and mercy knows no ethnic, national, racial, or gender boundaries. God chose Israel to be the special vehicle of God's revelation to all humanity, but Israel jumped to the wrong conclusion that God's plan of deliverance and redemption applied only to them.

When we first moved to Atlanta, I will admit, it was tough. We knew no one, and *man* did we think the people talked funny. There is nothing like an urban southern drawl. One of the things we did as we began Atlanta Youth Academy was establish a relationship with the school's founder, Larry Teem, outside of work. Larry was a privileged southern white man who represented everything that is completely different from me. He grew up in Buckhead in Atlanta, one of the wealthier parts of town, he went to a private school, and he was as southern as they come. Larry lived forty-five minutes away . . . on a *farm*. You could not have brought together two families from more different contexts. But Larry and I sat down and committed to having our families do dinner together once a month out at the farm. The farm had what I suppose all farms have: a barn, animals, and plenty of space. Larry and his wife, Lisa, live pretty simply and far away from city life. We were city people, straight outta Philly with our Northeast accents, loud and direct demeanor, and our horn-blowing, don't-stare-at-me-too-long selves.

Over the next four years we didn't miss many dinners together. They became a familiar place for our families to get to know and love each other outside of the mission that had brought us there. The dinners were a place for the Barber family to get to know deep southern culture and for the Teem family to get to know Northeast city culture. The meals were simple, but the time was precious and meaningful.

Those times helped us endure the struggles of mission together. They helped us understand and appreciate the humanity of the other. We learned to care for not just each other's position but each other's person. When we only know someone's position and roles, we can harm them. We easily forget that they were shaped by God and have families, dreams, and hopes. Getting to know real Atlantans helped us to overcome our stereotypes.

God may call us to go to Nineveh—a place we'd call hard. And God will speak to us there. We must not forget that those we consider the "Ninevites" are people, too. If we forget, we can wind up harming people in the name of our God. This is mission gone awry. Our Lord has plans for us to be bearers of good news in such spaces. But on the flip side, there is good news when we're marginalized and treated unjustly: there is a God of justice and peace for all people, who calls us to embrace all people. This God of justice will stand for us, and he loves us deeply and wants to know each of us.

What are the hard places in your life—those places you would rather not go out of fear or arrogance? The neighborhood you won't live in, or the church you won't go to? Is there a job you won't consider because it's not prestigious enough? To state it plainly, sometimes we think we are better than the people in these places. We don't see those people as fully human. We may also be just plain afraid. We think our lives may be in danger if we go to a certain side of town or travel to a different country. In our hard places, our faith is challenged and our desire for comfort is threatened. Sometimes the hard place is exactly where we need to be. Hard places push our buttons and bring out the prejudices that we aren't willing to face when we're in our own space. Hard places push us to trust and see God and others from a different perspective. God uses those places to enable us to know and love more deeply and to bring us closer to one another and to him. Throughout Scripture we see folks being called to hard places, so we ourselves should expect to be called as well.

Your hard place might be the city (or state or country) where you live and work. It might be a neighborhood your work takes you to every once in awhile, the office environment you've landed in, or your school or university setting. It might be a hospital or other institution where you find yourself waking up every morning. Your hard place might even be a jail or a prison. Regardless of where you are and why you're there, God is there as well. He has you in his care and has a mission for you there. The Dutch Reformed pastor and theologian Abraham Kuyper once declared, "There is not a square inch in the whole domain of our human existence over which Christ, who is Sovereign over *all*, does not cry, 'Mine!'" And as the Psalmist says it,

> Where can I go from your Spirit?
> Where can I flee from your presence?
> If I go up to the heavens, you are there;
> if I make my bed in the depths, you are there.
> If I rise on the wings of the dawn,
> if I settle on the far side of the sea,
> even there your hand will guide me,
> your right hand will hold me fast.
> If I say, "Surely the darkness will hide me
> and the light become night around me,"
> even the darkness will not be dark to you;
> the night will shine like the day,
> for darkness is as light to you. (Ps 139:7-12)

For much of American culture, there is a continual drive to improve our circumstances and to merely tolerate the place we find ourselves in until we can move on to a better job, a better home, a better church, a better neighborhood, a better state. Sometimes God does have a move in our future—a different place where he has kingdom work for us to do. But we need to live fully in the places where we already are and to which he has already led us, no matter how hard those places might be.

It's so difficult for us to embrace the call to go to hard places. We don't like moving out of our zones of comfort and influence. We only move forward when we feel it's safe. We have created a safe gospel that hinders the progress of peace and justice in the world. My friends, we are not called to *safe*. We never have been and we never will be. The Scriptures don't support safe—they support listening to the direction of God in our lives and moving forward into that reality. We can't reach hard people if we are avoiding the hard places. So the call isn't for safety; the call is for people of peace to reach out and embrace others in an effort to create change.

Sometimes we just have to go to the deep end and dive in. God will be present there if that's where he calls us. God can handle the struggle of the deep; our shallowness is what's really killing us. Diving in calls for an awful lot of trust in God and others and can be terrifying for many. But the current state in which we find ourselves across race and culture is already horrific. What would it look like to put a little more trust in the Creator?

2

THE ONES WE AVOID

Do not judge your neighbor until you have walked two moons in his moccasins.

Ancient proverb among the Cheyenne

Josh was a 6′4″ white dude, and when I first met him he opened both arms and said, "We're a hugging culture." There I was on the streets of Oakland, California, for the first time, and this large white dude was giving me a bear hug. My cultural antenna was up. I spent the rest of my weekend in Oakland trying to figure out whether I could work with this guy. He looked, thought, and approached things completely differently than I would. Everything from his teaching style to how he trained and talked to teams screamed of how different we were as leaders. We piled in his van to go somewhere and I thought, *There is no way I can work with this hippie.* He was explaining why soda was a waste of money and why the ministry wouldn't purchase it.

Josh and I went on to work together at Mission Year for the next seven years. Josh was director in Oakland and I was director in Atlanta. We would help shape an incredible ministry together, but we had our share of differences. He is a linear thinker and I am not. I'm an emotional person and Josh is subdued; when I felt the need to be louder and more expressive, his voice would get softer. But over those seven years, we became good friends and learned to appreciate each other's differences. And eventually our differences became the strength of our relationship. Although my first instinct was to back off, over time my heart and his became bound in friendship.

Many folks share that instinct to back off. We observe the behavior of others—or, worse, merely their looks, bearing, or choice of clothing—and make a judgment, even if only in our minds. From our judgments we create barriers, reasons for why we don't need to interact with certain individuals that cross our path. We're quick to dismiss others because learning to understand them would be difficult, time consuming, or painful, and we're slow to extend grace. We excuse our own oddities, misbehaviors, and lapses in judgment because we know the circumstances that forced us into them—but we reject the possibility that the other person might be able to point to the circumstances that led to their oddities, misbehaviors, or lapses in judgment. We like to keep others in their place—usually somewhere beneath us—and protect the high regard we have for ourselves.

Consider some of the following people. Do you find yourself having to deal with any of them?

- ***Those you just don't click with.*** These are the people that rub you the wrong way. You try to get along with them, but something doesn't jive, and it leads to really awkward moments.

You would much rather be with someone else. When you find yourself alone with them, the conversation seems forced because you have so little in common. But they're just as difficult in a group, especially if you really connect well with all the others in that circle.

- ***The disagreeable.*** These are the people you constantly disagree with. They see the world differently, and they have a different lifestyle from yours. It drives you completely nuts. You have very little in common. You butt heads on just about everything. You avoid them when possible, but because you share a set of friends, they remain a nagging presence in your life.
- ***The folks beneath you.*** These are the people that you always look down on—whether you admit it or not. You're not mean, but deep down you just don't think they're in your league—socially, educationally, economically, or whatever. They may not be bad people, but they are not on your level, and so you tolerate them at best.
- ***Control freaks.*** These are the people who don't ever want to listen. They don't have to, because they know it all and the best way to do it all. While this type of person can be a nuisance in your personal life, they can be a nightmare to deal with in a business environment and can ruin a team experience.
- ***Liars and backstabbers.*** To be successful you have to surround yourself with individuals you can trust and count on to be there for you. But you never know whether these people are lying or telling the truth. That type of uncertainty will wear you out quickly and tempt you to eliminate them from your life.

- ***Criminals.*** You might not want these people to be fully reconciled to society. Maybe they aren't worthy in your mind, or maybe you just don't want to take the trouble to make room for them. Reconciliation might be easier if the crime didn't happen to us, but what if we're the victims and we're forced to come face to face with the perpetrator?

We may think our lives are full of hard people like those represented on the list above. But we forget that there is another perspective through which we can see the people in and around our lives. We are called to a different perspective, a perspective that challenges us to embrace others instead of create boundaries. As followers of Christ, the perspective of embrace matters most. God has revealed to us through Scripture that we are called to love even those we'd rather avoid. So let's consider some of the hard people that Jesus embraced.

As a young Jewish man, Jesus wouldn't have naturally "clicked" with a tax collector like Zacchaeus. Something of a weasel, Zacchaeus was a Jew who had sold out to the Roman conquerors and obtained a position by which he could cheat his own people and amass wealth for himself. He was a friend of the empire of sorts. Who are the tax collectors in our lives? Many would name the police, a politician, or even a pastor who seems to care for power and prestige more than people. But Luke 19:1-10 describes how Jesus' respect and love for the sellouts turned Zacchaeus into a friend and an altogether better person.

Jesus seemed to come across disagreeable people all the time, but the Gerasene demoniac (Mk 5:1-20) was disagreeable in his own way. His life was dominated by evil spirits, and he had somehow lost control. This dude was loud and belligerent, and so strong that he could break chains and defeat any number of men that came against him. Everyone else avoided him at all costs, but Jesus interacted with him lovingly, healed him, and made him a friend.

Every Jew in Jesus' day viewed Samaritans with contempt and from a position of superiority. To the Jews, the Samaritans, a mixed-race people descended from the Jews, were compromisers, impure and wayward. This perspective was so much a part of the Jewish psyche that Jesus' own disciples marveled that he would take them into Samaria rather than skirting around it, and they were even more amazed when they found him conversing with a woman there. Jesus had sought this particular woman out so that he could treat her with respect and offer her the true, abundant life that he came to bring. Through her witness, many in her town came to believe (Jn 4:1-45).

As for control freaks, the Pharisees had something like 618 regulations in addition to God's law to ensure that the Jews wouldn't find themselves on the wrong side of God's law (or their own interpretation of it). And yet Jesus sought them out, reasoned with them, and patiently tried to love them into his kingdom.

Jesus had an untrustworthy backstabber, Judas Iscariot, within his closest circle of friends. Though he apparently knew all along that Judas would eventually betray him, Jesus always dealt with Judas as he did with his other disciples—lovingly, gently, patiently.

What about criminals? At his darkest hour, as Jesus hung dying on a Roman cross, he took the time to offer hope and encouragement to a convicted thief. At a time when anyone else would have been completely self-absorbed, Jesus was still outward-focused, directing his compassion toward one of the lowest members of society, a confessed criminal, someone he could have easily despised.

Can God really love everyone? And can the same really be expected from us? Intellectually we can acknowledge this truth, but our actions are sometimes contrary. Let's admit that we often fail to emulate our Lord when it comes to the hard people in our lives, and that, depending on the degree of relational difficulty, we tend to either tolerate such individuals or avoid them at all costs.

TRIBAL PREJUDICE

It's one thing to acknowledge that there are individuals who are difficult to love. But if we're honest, we'll find that we also cling to prejudices about entire categories of people—we consider them as somehow less than those in our own tribe. This practice is so widespread that we're used to hearing claims that illustrate this all the time. For example:

- Women are worse drivers than men.
- Native Americans lack ambition.
- Renters aren't as smart as homeowners.
- Dark skin is less attractive than light skin.
- Urbanites are less sophisticated than suburbanites.
- Poor people are just plain lazy.
- Iraqis love conflict and violence.
- Undocumented immigrants are a drain on the economy.
- People from Appalachia are backward.

You get the idea. We have a whole arsenal of prejudices ready to aim at whoever crosses our path. What's more, we can easily find others of our own tribe who are willing to confirm and encourage us in these stereotypes of others. Isn't that the whole point of a racist, sexist, or ethnic joke? By laughing together at a scenario that demeans another group, we reinforce and justify our own feelings of superiority as a group.

You don't need me to tell you that this tendency—of which we're all guilty—is not loving, that it doesn't lead to peace and harmony, that it's not what Jesus modeled and demanded of his followers. The fact that you're taking time to read this book means that you're open to examining and improving your interactions with others. But maybe your personal prejudices seem relatively harmless. You don't act upon them; in fact, you really don't have much opportunity to interact at all with those others—because for the most part, we all tend to surround ourselves with people who look like we do, think like we do, and share our tastes in music, sports, politics, and religion.

But let me suggest that prejudice is not so benign. As the daily news reminds us, our world is full of hatred, violence, murder, and war. And in the majority of cases, the victim is separated from the perpetrator by differences in gender, race, religion, culture, or nationality. That is, the violence that continues to erupt all around us has as its basis the very same prejudices that we harbor, accept, tolerate, and cultivate in ourselves and among our own tribes. There's nothing wrong with having a tribe, but when your tribe begins to dictate their own culture as normative for all tribes and damage and harm others, it feeds injustice and oppression.

It's really easy to think that undocumented immigrants should be deported until we get to know a mom of Mexican descent who faces the possibility of being separated from her children. When the black male who is accused or shot is our son's friend and has visited our house, our attitudes toward law and justice will be different. When a Muslim helps our kid understand math or is the nurse who cared for our sick parent, our views will begin to shift because humanity and closeness overcome hate.

What is it that drives us away from one another? Why don't we embrace more? We seem to forget that God made us all and that by embracing we may in fact enhance who we are as humans. We must remember people aren't philosophies to be discussed. People are to be embraced, loved, cherished, supported, celebrated, and appreciated no matter how difficult they may be or how different they seem. There is no hierarchy of human being. Our color, gender, culture, economic level, educational achievements, or religion never makes us better than another person.

LOVING THE UNLOVABLE

I have made a commitment to love people. I firmly believe that the decision to love whoever God places in our lives really changes things. We may not always get to eat what we want or to listen to the music that we prefer (something that minority communities have done throughout history), but when we work to embrace others and other cultures, we can more deeply participate in our shared call to be friends and coworkers in the kingdom of Christ.

Granted, we ought to be able to overlook differences in musical taste, gender, and skin color. But what about the really hard people? Aren't some people—our real enemies—so arrogant, hateful, violent, and unchangeably difficult that we can be excused for not loving them? Surely there's a limit to the type of people God expects us to love. Aren't some people just plain unlovable?

Let's look again at the children of Israel during their exile in Babylon. They had every reason to hate the Babylonians, the people who had conquered and enslaved them. The Israelites who had survived the Babylonian brutality—the murder of their friends and children and the destruction of their homes—would have had the images of those atrocities seared in their memories. They would have wanted God to avenge them by visiting destruction on their captors. I'm not speculating here. That sentiment is recorded by one of the exiles in Psalm 137:

> Daughter Babylon, doomed to destruction,
> happy is the one who repays you
> according to what you have done to us.
> Happy is the one who seizes your infants
> and dashes them against the rocks. (Ps 137:8-9)

There was almost certainly a feeling of religious superiority in this. The captives were God's chosen people, and their captors were pagan barbarians. But whether or not this religious superiority was justified, certainly the bitter anger expressed in this psalm had a basis in righteousness, right? Doesn't the fact that this sentiment was recorded in Scripture mean that God condoned the desire for revenge? As history records, the Babylonians would in fact be punished by the one true God.

While this is an extreme example, doesn't it demonstrate that it's okay for us not to love everyone, that there are some people we are not required to try to understand, forgive, and live with peacefully? Are there some categories of people that are outside of God's compassion and so outside of ours? God's message to the exiles in Jeremiah provides the answer to all these questions: "Seek the peace and prosperity of the city to which I have carried you into exile. Pray to the Lord for it, because if it prospers, you too will prosper" (Jer 29:7).

Let me mention four insights I find here (I'll flesh them out in later chapters). First, the Lord doesn't condone or praise the desire for revenge. The Psalms record the entire range of human emotions, and their inclusion in Scripture does not imply God's approval of them. Instead, the Bible makes it clear that God's ways are not our ways. Elsewhere, God warns against harboring anger and hatred and reserves for himself the role of avenger (Rom 12:19). Second, even Babylon is worthy of God's compassion. The Lord does not share our hatred and prejudices, no matter how right we think they are. Third, the Lord's command to pray for Babylon reminds us that his blessing can come upon any nation through the prayers and actions of his people.

All three of these insights can be found in Jonah's story as well. The people of Nineveh were just as bad a bunch as the Babylonians: idolatrous murderers who oppressed and enslaved. The Lord called Jonah to warn these evil folks that they were incurring his wrath, and when they repented, he showed them compassion and mercy. Jonah connects the dots so we can't miss the picture of God's character: "Isn't this what I said, Lord, when I was still at home? That is what I tried to forestall by fleeing to Tarshish. I knew that you are a gracious and compassionate God, slow to anger and abounding in love, a God who relents from sending calamity" (Jon 4:2).

The fourth insight may be the hardest for us to accept. And that is that we and every other person—regardless of race, gender, socioeconomic status, nationality, or religion—are on the same level: that of the created. God alone is the sovereign Creator. We're all on the same playing field—even with the most difficult people imaginable.

NO FAVORITISM WITH GOD

The first-century church struggled with issues of ethnicity too. Arguably, the main drama recorded in the book of Acts had to do with questions about ethnic and religious categorization. And the first such question was about whether the good news of the resurrection of Jesus and the establishment of God's kingdom on earth even applied to those who weren't Jews.

The majority view among the Jews who saw Jesus' resurrection as proof that he was their promised Messiah was that this Messiah was only for them. They believed that people from all the other nations were beyond redeeming, that they were outside of God's favor, love, and mercy. But as Philip, the Samaritan woman, Paul, and others were given divine appointments to share the gospel with people from these other nations, these outsiders embraced the good news about Jesus and repented of their own sin. And what's more, the Holy Spirit manifested in their lives in the same way as the Jewish believers.

Peter was one of the first Jews to understand God's perspective about people from other nations. God led Peter to this new way of thinking—he visited Peter in a dream and then sent a righteous and respectable, God-fearing Roman military officer to him. Peter expressed what he learned through all this in Acts 10:34-35: "I now realize how true it is that God does not show favoritism but accepts from every nation the one who fears him and does what is right." His conclusion holds even in our modern times of racial, national, and religious turmoil.

WORK TO DO

God loves even the people we find hard to like. Christ calls us to follow his example, to love the "least of these," the people we'd rather avoid, the ones in those categories that we've put labels on and barriers around. We each have a lot of work to do if we are to obey our Lord and heed the call to be ministers of reconciliation in a conflicted world. As long as we allow barriers of prejudice to stand between us and hard individuals or between us and whole categories of people, we cannot become the agents of peace we are meant to be. We must begin by asking God for supernatural love for people of all kinds. We must be willing to examine and repent of our own treasured prejudices. And we must be willing to enter into deep relationships with the individuals and categories of people that we find most difficult to love.

My friends, the loss is huge when we let our prejudices lead the way. We are all made in the image of God, and when we don't see that in each other we lose sight of God himself. When some are excluded, hurt, oppressed, ignored, tossed aside, dismissed easily, and made invisible because of our prejudices and racism, we lose God. Our light grows dim and our paths become clouded with judgment, suspicion, violence. Today we have inequality in schools, mass incarceration, police brutality, sex trafficking, terrorist acts—these are all consequences of our prejudices and racism rooted in our lack of acceptance of the other.

I recently spoke at a church in Buffalo on the effects of mass incarceration and had the opportunity to talk with a woman whose husband formerly had been incarcerated and now could not find work. Heartbroken, she talked about how good of a father, leader, and husband he had become after being released sixteen years ago. This man has been transformed, but people still will not hire him. This family lives with hurt caused by the rejection they face from potential employers. The label that he carries affects his family's joy almost daily. What a gift and story we all miss when we fail to embrace someone formerly incarcerated whose life has been changed. The image of the Creator becomes a bit dimmer in our communities because of the people and stories that are missing. How much longer are we going to look past the light of the *imago Dei* in each person?

If we are going to avoid this loss, we've got to be intentional about doing the hard work to know, understand, and love the other. This is vital. While we have to realize that this is a process and that it takes time, we also have to commit to preventing harm toward others even while we're in process. A no-harm commitment means that as you are learning and moving toward understanding that it may be important for you to speak out even though you aren't fully versed.

Bessie and Lisa worked together for years at the same hospital. They had a cordial relationship and would often have conversations about their sons, who were both teenagers. Bessie is black and Lisa is white. They were both single parents and raising their boys on their own. One day Bessie got the call no mom ever wants. Her son had been shot on the corner and was headed to the hospital. Bessie left work immediately to get across town and see her son. When Bessie arrived at the hospital, she found out that her son had died. The death of Bessie's son was shocking and devastating to the entire staff that worked with her each day. We knew her son: we'd heard stories about him, laughed about his mistakes, and celebrated his accomplishments. Bessie was so proud of him. He was a handsome young man—a high school student with a great smile and personality. What we did not expect was Lisa's reaction. Lisa took it upon herself to arrange care for Bessie and her daughter as they grieved. Even though Lisa lived in a different part of town and had a different life experience, she put herself in Bessie's place. She reached across race and class lines to grieve deeply with Bessie.

Supporting a friend of color as they grieve a police shooting says to your friend *I may not understand everything but because you hurt, I hurt with you.* If we don't speak, it harms; it says *I'm going to keep my distance.* It says *You are not my friend.* Like Lisa, we can learn to support others and suffer with others even when we aren't personally able to relate.

If we want to learn to see the light of the *imago Dei* in each person and avoid a major loss, we need to put ourselves in new contexts where we can learn from the other. Social spaces are crucial. Take a trip to the movies on the other side of town or go to a high school basketball game there. Go see a football game at an HBCU (Historically Black Colleges and Universities) school and experience the band and community. Take your children to the museum on a reservation, or do an arts walk in the Chinatown of your city.

We can also learn to see others and avoid major loss by listening to and telling stories. Story is a powerful gift. When we get the chance to hear other people's stories, we can connect with their feelings and begin to see them as real people. Through listening to the stories, we can become fully present in others' moments. This is a gift we share as human beings, but sadly a gift seldom used. Stories can bring us closer to one another and enable us to participate in the love Peter writes about when he says, "Above all, love each other deeply, because love covers over a multitude of sins" (1 Pet 4:8).

3

GOD LIKES PUMPKIN PIE

"For my thoughts are not your thoughts,
neither are your ways my ways," declares the LORD.
"For as the heavens are higher than the earth,
so are my ways higher than your ways
and my thoughts than your thoughts."

Isaiah 55:8-9

It was close to Thanksgiving, and in my high school cafeteria there was a special meal to celebrate. A high school cafeteria in the late '70s left a lot to be desired, but that week there was turkey, stuffing, cranberry sauce, potatoes, and, for dessert, pie. I walked through the line and sampled everything, but when I got to the pie, I read *pumpkin pie*, and a strange look came across my face. I had never seen pumpkin pie before. I asked the person behind the counter, "What does pumpkin pie taste like?" and I heard, "Have you never had pumpkin pie?" When I said no, the person behind the counter and the other students in line began to laugh hysterically. One of the students said, "What, do black people not eat pumpkins? It's one of the main dishes for Thanksgiving!"

I was in the ninth grade, so I was super embarrassed. I refused the pie, which made them laugh even more. I had no idea what pumpkin tasted like, and I didn't know a single black person who ate pumpkin pie. I don't know many who eat it today.

SEEING PEOPLE THROUGH GOD'S EYES

So here's what's wrong with much of our world today—the explanation for the racial tension in our own country and for the ethnic and religious wars around the globe: although we each have a unique set of perspectives, we expect everyone else to share those same perspectives. Even though the sum total of our own beliefs, values, likes, and dislikes is utterly unique to us, we can seem disappointed or offended when we discover that others don't share our exact view of the world. It's like the assumption that everyone eats pumpkin pie at Thanksgiving or that everyone even celebrates Thanksgiving. My Native friends would see the special cafeteria food completely different than I do, and Thanksgiving is just another day to much of the world. God is doing much more than Thanksgiving on the last Thursday in November. (He may be watching the Dallas Cowboys, but that's a different story.)

In extreme cases, these expectations can lead to isolation—individuals who just don't get along with anyone, who keep to themselves or blunder through society clashing with everyone they meet. More often, we succeed in finding others who share important parts of our perspectives, and we base our friendships on that. This only reinforces our belief that our own set of perspectives is the only correct set. But whose story of Thanksgiving is correct—the colonists' or Native Americans'?

There's an even bigger problem, and that's when we begin to make our own perspectives—our assumptions and biases, our likes and dislikes—part of our theology. We're tempted to believe that the way *we* think about people and places is the way *God* sees them. We may not voice this idea, but it lingers there in our thoughts, and it comes out in our actions and interactions. When we assume that God agrees with our perspectives, we provide ourselves with religious justification for our thoughts and behaviors, no matter how divisive or intolerant those thoughts and behaviors might be, and that's dangerous. "Surely," we might say, "Thanksgiving is a day we thank God for family and this country."

I think we understand this problem when it comes to other people and other groups. It's obvious that al-Qaeda militants are mistaken in believing that their terrorism has God's blessing behind it. It seems pretty clear that in the battle for the disputed lands in Palestine, someone (or everyone) is wrong in their conviction that God is wholly on their side and totally opposed to their opponent's goals.

But when it comes to ourselves—individually and as a tribe—aren't we pretty much blind to the possibility that God sees things differently than we do? Or have we made a habit of pausing long enough to think about how God might correct our thinking about that hard place or those difficult people? We would probably affirm that as followers of Christ we want to see the world through heavenly eyes. But are we open to letting this actually change us? Are we willing to deal with our favorite prejudices, the fears we cling to most dearly, and our favorite misconceptions about other people?

Before we go any further, it's important for us think about some of the many ways in which God's perspectives might differ from ours. This will be the chapter where we go into deeper theological and philosophical waters. Well, okay, they're not really so deep, but the fact is that we seldom even wade into such waters, even when they have a lot of relevance for our daily lives.

By the way, I *have* tried pumpkin pie and although I prefer sweet potato pie, both are good and enjoyable. Have you tried the other pie? One may not be your preference, but cultural perspectives are good to share.

CREATOR AND CREATED

The most basic difference between God and us is our very being—we are created and God is the Creator. It's hard to overstate what this means. And yet our certainty in the rightness of our own views depends, in part, on our pretending that there's not really that big a difference between God and us.

Scripture tells us otherwise.

The Bible opens with an account of God creating the universe out of nothing. The main theme of this ancient story is that God is completely different from all created things. Humanity shares with all the rest of the universe—stars and planets, seas and mountains, and all other living things—the dependence of the created on the One who creates and sustains. This idea is repeated in Psalm 104, which is a poetic parallel of the Genesis 1 narrative:

> All creatures look to you
>   to give them their food at the proper time.
> When you give it to them,
>   they gather it up;
> when you open your hand,
>   they are satisfied with good things.
> When you hide your face,
>   they are terrified;

when you take away their breath,
  they die and return to the dust.
When you send your Spirit,
  they are created,
  and you renew the face of the ground. (Ps 104:27-30)

Indeed, in all the major creation passages in Scripture, God is portrayed as wholly other than us and every created thing.

This is also the main message of God's long discourse with Job (Job 38–41), and it has particular relevance to our discussion here. Job found himself in a hard space, having lost all that he had: family, belongings, and even good health. And he found himself surrounded by hard people: friends who were acting as anything but friends. Job had some sincere and reasonable questions as he tried to make sense of what was happening to him. He was ultimately comforted by the simple fact that God showed up, a reminder to Job of the Lord's love and faithfulness. But when God showed up, the content of his message was to remind Job of the vast difference between their perspectives:

Where were you when I laid the earth's foundation?
  Tell me, if you understand.
Who marked off its dimensions? Surely you know!
  Who stretched a measuring line across it?
On what were its footings set,
  or who laid its cornerstone—
while the morning stars sang together
  and all the angels shouted for joy? (Job 38:4-7)

In Romans 9, Paul illustrates this distinction quite powerfully with an analogy:

> But who are you, a human being, to talk back to God? Shall what is formed say to the one who formed it, "Why did you make me like this?" Does not the potter have the right to make out of the same lump of clay some pottery for special purposes and some for common use? (Rom 9:20-21)

We might use another analogy for this: God is the author of an epic drama and we are characters in it. We play the roles written for us, responding to cues from the actors and actresses with whom we share the stage. We say our lines and follow the stage directions found in the script, perhaps even improvising here and there. It would be foolish if we dared to claim that we had a perfect understanding of the entire drama and of the role of the other characters. Doesn't God have a better perspective of such things, one that makes our small perspectives seem rather naive and insignificant?

God's perspective about the people and places in our lives is much different than our perspective. This difference is beautiful because it shows us the vastness of God as Creator—the pumpkin pie, sweet potato pie–loving God. But our shameful denial of God's authoritative perspective as Creator has led to chaos. We just don't see each other how he sees each of us. God is saddened by our lack of respect when we fail to see his image in the other.

DIFFERENT TIME ZONES

Related to the Creator-creature difference is a temporal difference, a difference in time. We're stuck (for now) in a single dimension of time. We can't change the past, the decisions we've made, and the actions we took there. We can't see the future with any clarity, but we can work to shape it by the way we live in the present. Just as our present is shaped by the past, our present decisions and actions have significant implications for the future. Depending on how we deal with the hard situations we find ourselves in today and the difficult people around us now, we have the potential to shape a better future.

But God is not confined to our single dimension of time because he does not experience time in the same way that we do. Moses declares of God,

> A thousand years in your sight
> are like a day that has just gone by,
> or like a watch in the night. (Ps 90:4)

Peter in the New Testament echoes this: "But do not forget this one thing, dear friends," he says. "With the Lord a day is like a thousand years, and a thousand years are like a day" (2 Pet 3:8). Time, as we experience it, is a dimension of this universe, a part of this creation. God created the time we experience, and God is transcendent to (or outside of) time.

Of course, God enters into history and deals with humanity in our time. Jesus experienced time just as all other humans always have. But the point is that God is not bound by time as we are. I know this can be hard for us to understand, but I think it's important that we try. God knows how the epic drama ends. This can be hard to swallow because of the way we fumble over the scene in which we're currently acting. It's very hard to swallow because of the devastation we see in the world where we live today. The present time is painful in so many ways for so many people, yet there are people who continue to hope and rely on the greater good that will be realized. We hope for a return to that creation story where everything created has value as it was given by our beautiful Creator God.

The Bible tells us that God's plan for our salvation and redemption—involving Christ's incarnation, the cross, and the resurrection—was planned from before time began. Ephesians 1:4 describes this as "before the creation of the world," and Titus 1:2 and 2 Timothy 1:9 place it "before the beginning of time." We need to understand that God makes "known the end from the beginning" (Is 46:10). We don't know the future, but God does. We can't see how the problems of this hard place are ever going to be set right, but we trust that our actions are connected to the reconciling work of the God of the universe. Sometimes we can't imagine how these relationships could ever be worked out, or how we could ever get along with the "other" people, but know that redemption is already a present reality in Christ. We need to apply ourselves to the work of justice for those suffering in our time while we acknowledge that we only know a small part of the story.

The life of the Jewish patriarch Joseph provides a good illustration of this. We know the end of Joseph's story and how the Lord used Joseph's position in the Egyptian Pharaoh's court to sustain and nurture a nation. And while we know the end of Joseph's story because it's already passed, the Lord knew the end of the story because his being is not confined by time.

But think for a minute about how Joseph experienced his life. Talk about hard places and hard people! He was sold into slavery by his own brothers. He spent years in prison because he was accused by a lying witness. Most of his life was spent in a foreign land that he would not have chosen among people who were not his people. And yet God was with him in those hard places. And God used those hard relationships for the benefit and rescue of everyone in the story. And God was not surprised by the happy outcome.

I am not saying that we should accept current situations of injustice. I *am* saying that we know that God hates these situations and that he *will* move them forward toward freedom. Wouldn't it have been great for Joseph if the Lord had assured him all along, as he was suffering through hard times, that his story would end happily? More to the point, wouldn't it be wonderful if the Lord would give us today an assurance that he'll use the hard places and the hard people in our lives to bring about a good outcome for all of us? He did and he does.

The account of Joseph's life (Gen 37, 39–50) makes it clear that the Lord continually reassured Joseph of his love. When Joseph landed in prison, Scripture tells us that "the LORD was with Joseph and showed him steadfast love" (Gen 39:21 ESV). This idea is repeated at each of the hard places in Joseph's story.

Likewise, a vast number of biblical promises apply directly to us and are meant to reassure us of God's purpose and control when we find ourselves in difficult circumstances, in hard places, surrounded by tough people. Probably because of its breadth of application and its clarity, a favorite promise to Christians has been from Romans 8:28: "And we know that in all things God works for the good of those who love him, who have been called according to his purpose." This is a huge promise, and if we could continuously hold fast to it, it would transform the way we approach the hard places and hard relationships to which God calls us. The promise doesn't keep us from difficulty but gives us hope in its midst.

DIFFERENT PRIORITIES

Joseph's story offers us another important truth: God's priorities are not the same as ours.

Admit it. We're pretty much all about things like personal comfort, health, pleasure, and financial security. Sure, we have many other good values: relationships, education, integrity, and such. But our day-to-day and moment-to-moment decisions and actions are often filtered first through the grid of immediate comfort and security. We do things because we feel like doing them, and we don't do other things because we don't. And we live in a culture that encourages us in this self-absorbed approach to life. The economics of our global consumer culture depend on training each of us to make a priority of our own pleasure, comfort, and self-image. So we see the world through the lens of our own self-gratification.

In a world where perspectives and stories are varied but where the media and other forms of mass communication dictate the agenda and try to shape what we see as important, we need to resist a single narrative. We need to resist a narrative that tells us that God's ways are the same as the ways of the dominant culture. We need to resist a narrative that isn't shaped by our relationships with one another in all our varied perspectives and stories. Relationships save us from prioritizing our own comfort and pleasure to the detriment of the other—even after Joseph's brothers treated him with murderous disdain, his familial ties moved him to help them.

ALL ABOUT RELATIONSHIPS

The differences between God and us are important distinctions that affect our perspectives and our priorities. But there is a characteristic we share with our Creator, a similarity between us and our Maker, that is of great importance to how we relate to hard people.

Before the universe was created, God existed as a relational being. God was self-sufficient and complete and did not need anyone else to love or be loved by. This is because God has always (from eternity past) existed as a Trinity, a single being of three persons, Father, Son, and Holy Spirit. Scripture makes it clear that God is love; that essential attribute makes sense (even prior to creation) because the very being of God is completely relational.

We humans—male and female—are made in the image of that triune God. And while the *imago Dei* in us has many aspects, it's clear that we are relational beings. We were created out of relationship and for relationship; we're relational at our core. We cannot help but function in community, and when we're not in community, we suffer consequences. We were made to be together, and that's by God's design. Human flourishing requires that we establish, mend, and maintain relationships with other people.

Jesus exemplified and taught that those loving relationships ought to cross culture's artificial boundaries of politics, ethnicity, nationality, gender, and socioeconomic status. But in our world today, we have become adept at erecting and fortifying these barriers. We live in the most individualistic society in history, and when we do interact with others, we do our best to make sure that those people look, talk, think, and behave just as we do. These tendencies may keep us in our comfort zones, but they are antithetical to God's will for us. They are the enemy of God's plan of redemption and relationship, and they keep us distant from one another and ultimately from the one who created us.

This does not mean that ethnic identity is not important. Ethnic identity gives us a sense of belonging and place that's unique. God created us uniquely and that should be honored. But he did not create us to be exclusive and closed off to one another. We display the full character of our Creator together. Any piece missing, distorted, or betrayed is a perversion of God's image.

SEEING THROUGH GOD'S EYES

Christ came to earth to heal and redeem the four relationships broken at the fall—between us and God, between us and ourselves, between us and other people, and between us and the rest of creation. Right relationships are God's main priority, and it's through right relationship with God that we are healed. Jesus calls us *friend*. The Father calls us *sons and daughters*. The Holy Spirit is with us as we go through life, calling us into deeper intimacy with God and with others.

Is it possible for us to see each other the way God sees us instead of through our biases? The truth is that God doesn't see people the way we do, no matter how much we try to convince ourselves and others that our way is the Creator's way. In God's eyes, each and every person is a bearer of his image. Each is a special creation, each is loved, each is in need of God's love and forgiveness.

God doesn't play favorites and he doesn't love one person more than another. He loves each person perfectly. If anything, God operates counter to our usual approach—no going after the rich and famous, the movers and shakers, the people in the "in" crowd. Jesus reached out to the margins of society to make sure that those who were overlooked, ostracized, and treated unjustly knew that they were loved. As ambassadors for the kingdom of God, we need to begin to see others as Christ does—as people in need of the same divine love, mercy, and grace that has been extended to us.

TIDE TURNED

I remember when I first started out serving the homeless in Philly. Donna and I were going to downtown Philly with blankets and hot soup in the cold of winter, and sandwiches with cold drinks in the summer. We saw God do some miraculous things among such vulnerable people.

Although I believe my call was authentic and what Donna and I were doing each night was right, to me homeless people were just people to be helped. They needed to be off drugs, helped with mental illness—or they were just plain lazy and my work was to enlighten them. I didn't treat them poorly, but my internal attitude was not one of honor. I didn't notice that attitude, but it was there. I didn't discover it until the evening when our van caught on fire and I sat on the steps of the central library weeping. The homeless men that I thought needed me gave me a lesson on love that changed me forever. They gathered around to pray for me. They sat with me and spoke encouraging words to me. One person brought me a drink. These people were not the people I thought they were, and I was not the person they thought I was. The tide turned, and they comforted me that night.

It really is a good thing they were not who I believed they were and that they were who God created them to be. They loved me—based on the relationship we were establishing—without conditions or judgment. They were not the mentally ill, lazy people I judged them to be, but rather loving people who knew how to care for someone hurting. It was then that I learned to respect all people no matter their circumstances. My thoughts about certain people had developed through a particular theological and cultural perspective that was flawed, and I needed to learn. My teachers lived on the streets without homes.

It really is a good thing that God's thoughts are not mine—that he doesn't think like me—because so many people would be written off wrongly. It's a good thing his ways are not my ways. If it were up to me, my van would not have burned up that evening, but because of it, I learned something priceless. I don't know what to think of all the things that happen in the world. I struggle with the evil things I see happening to people. I am not for injustice of any kind, but I know I've learned lessons through some difficult things. I don't always know God's ways—and in fact I struggle with them many times—but I am thankful they are not my ways because I am sure the world would be much worse.

MAKING THE OTHER PIE A ROUTINE

When I met my wife I wasn't really into theater, but she was. One Saturday when we were in college I found myself at Carnegie Hall in New York listening to her sing with Temple University's concert choir. She seemed to be so alive before, during, and after the concert that it piqued my interest. I needed to know this part of her and learn more about it. So I started watching films I had no interest in but were her favorites such as *Fiddler on the Roof* and *A Raisin in the Sun*. I made a practice of watching or going to performances, and eventually I fell in love with theater for myself. Now I love theater. I take in as many plays as possible and go to a Broadway show every chance I can get. It's something we now enjoy together.

I fell in love by making it a routine. We can grow to love each other when we commit to embrace something new as a learner and as part of our routines. We must place ourselves into a common space to learn from the other—not as an event but as way of living. Unity takes work. The more we expose ourselves to each other the more we will fall in love with each other. I recommend creating space in your life to hear someone different and to be immersed into a different space. Go to a black church or a church of another cultural background once a month, sit in a mass, be taught by a woman, attend a sweat lodge, or do whatever represents a foreign experience to you, and do it routinely.

May we, Christ's followers of this generation, catch a glimpse of—and work toward—the unity for which Jesus prayed while on earth!

> I'm praying not only for them
> But also for those who will believe in me
> Because of them and their witness about me.
> The goal is for all of them to become one heart and mind—
> Just as you, Father, are in me and I in you,
> So they might be one heart and mind with us.
> Then the world might believe that you, in fact, sent me.
> The same glory you gave me, I gave them,
> So they'll be as unified and together as we are—
> I in them and you in me.
> Then they'll be mature in this oneness,
> And give the godless world evidence
> That you've sent me and loved them
> In the same way you've loved me.
>
> Father, I want those you gave me
> To be with me, right where I am,
> So they can see my glory, the splendor you gave me,
> Having loved me

Long before there ever was a world.
Righteous Father, the world has never known you,
But I have known you, and these disciples know
That you sent me on this mission.
I have made your very being known to them—
Who you are and what you do—
And continue to make it known,
So that your love for me
Might be in them
Exactly as I am in them. (Jn 17:20-26 The Message)

4

LOOKING AT CHANGE THE RIGHT WAY

But now in Christ Jesus you who once were far away have been brought near by the blood of Christ.

Ephesians 2:13

All this is from God, who reconciled us to himself through Christ and gave us the ministry of reconciliation.

2 Corinthians 5:18

This message was forwarded to me from a friend after the Baltimore uprising over the death of Freddie Gray:

> Hi Josh. I had a conversation on Facebook with one of your friends who lives in Oregon concerning watching young black men in my neighborhood. He was offended because I told him that if his sons walked through the neighborhood I would look at them with caution since most of the crime has been committed by young black

> men. I have searched your Facebook page back to last year and can't find the post. I guess it was deleted. Can you message him and let him know that I am sorry? I now realize how bigoted, shallow, and discriminating it is for me to think that way. The Baltimore riots and conversation has broadened how I see and feel about my black friends and neighbors. As a white man, I hadn't noticed the privilege I get just for my skin color. I didn't realize that to be black is a struggle in so many ways in this country. I foolishly thought that we're all human beings, and that we all have the same opportunities no matter what color we are. I now know this isn't true. I realized that I don't have to defend myself as a good white person when the black community is frustrated, angry, and crying out for justice. I now realize my prejudices, and I want your friend in Oregon to know this. Please tell him that I won't judge his sons and that I won't judge my young black neighbors anymore. I will do my best to be a part of bringing healing. Please ask your friend in Oregon to forgive me. I don't want to be another white man who doesn't get it.

These words came to me a year after this same gentleman, Andy, was a retractor on a Facebook post I made about the tragedy of black men being killed by police. Andy's initial declaration was that he would look at my two sons like they were criminals. It was a personal indictment. But Andy lives in Baltimore and his heart began to change as the black community—his neighbors in Baltimore—began suffering. I had been a distant voice on Facebook, but when things erupted in Andy's own city with people he knew, his racism changed to solidarity. It doesn't always seem like change is coming, but sometimes it surprises us: Andy is now an advocate.

DANGEROUS EXPECTATIONS

We have so many expectations for the people in our lives. Our desire for these expectations to be met is incredibly strong and when they aren't we become disappointed, disillusioned, or hurt to varying degrees. We put a lot of stock in our relationships; our friends mean a lot us and we count on them to live up to our standards.

But there are two expectations that I think are more dangerous than others: the expectation that someone will change, or its converse, that someone will not change. These kinds of expectations can create major stumbling blocks in our relationships. Let's explore three stories that illustrate this issue.

Lucy's story. Lucy, a white woman, was committed to ministry—living and serving in a black neighborhood—and she began the year full of hope. But Lucy's year had not been as great as she had expected. She kept running into roadblocks with her neighbors. In our monthly talks she expressed deep frustration with how her relationships were moving forward, and she was close to leaving. She had become very cynical and started to make some statements that bordered on racist. When she expressed disbelief that one of her neighbors hadn't changed a particular behavior, some lights went off for me. Lucy had met her neighbors and then promptly decided they needed to change. She decided that whatever they were doing and how they were doing it was not acceptable, and when her neighbors did not change over time she became disillusioned with them and with God. Her cynicism was rooted in the standards she had put on her neighbors, standards that took away some of the authenticity of her relationships with them. Many of Lucy's standards were deeply rooted in her culture. She was disturbed by things like being late, their diets, the cleanliness of their homes, what they let their children watch, how they talked to one another, and on and on.

If we enter relationships with the expectation that the other person will take on our values, we're on the wrong road. This road starts with judgment and can end in complete breakdown. Lucy had to figure this out the hard way, but she did eventually change her expectations. When she did, she was able to be with and enjoy her neighbors for who they were and not for who she expected them to become. Those times with her neighbors allowed her to embrace them authentically. The need for them to change fell away and was replaced with a desire for deeper friendship—friendship she's still enjoying many years later.

Harry's story. Harry is a good guy. He loves meeting new people and learning about new cultures. Harry, who is white, met Louis, who is Hispanic, and they started a friendship. Harry and Louis went to games together, hung out a couple of times a week, and genuinely enjoyed one another's company. But a year into the friendship, Harry came to me and asked what I could do to help him with his struggling friendship with Louis. He began to explain how they had been such good friends and loved each other, but that lately Louis had seemed to change. He was now challenging Harry around race and culture just about every time they got together. "It makes me uncomfortable," Harry said. "I need to take a break from him. We disagree so much now." Harry related that when he and Louis first met, Louis would go along with Harry and not question him much. But a month before Harry and I spoke, a close friend of Louis's dad had been deported. This man had been here in the States for many years and raised his children here and then was suddenly separated from his family. This changed Louis's view about culture, race, and even being an American. The change was too much for Harry. This hadn't been part of their friendship before and now, suddenly, it was front and center.

We have to be ready for unexpected change in others that causes our friendships to change too. Committing to love someone means committing to them even when changes occur—even the changes you can't begin to understand because they come from a place you haven't been.

Philemon's story. I love the story of Philemon because it captures this idea of change well. Paul writes to Philemon, a wealthy businessman of the time, to let him know that one of his slaves, Onesimus—who had stolen from Philemon and run away—is now a brother in Christ and has been extremely helpful in Paul's work. Paul tells Philemon that if Onesimus owes him anything that he should charge it to Paul's account. (Then he goes on to say that—oh yeah, Philemon—you owe me your life.) Philemon now had to relate to Onesimus as a brother and not as a slave or a thief. I can imagine that Onesimus was a hard person for Philemon to embrace. Though the change in Onesimus was good it probably challenged Philemon deeply.

Whether we are Philemon or Onesimus, these kinds of changes catch us by surprise and ask us to relate to the other differently. Change is difficult. Accepting a new way of relating to someone is overwhelming. But the work has to be done, no matter how daunting the situation. New places and new situations bring forth life, freedom, and hope where it may have been absent. Change can bring justice, peace, and opportunity as we embrace each other's stories.

When we encounter situations in which we feel changes are needed, what often needs to change is not the other person but ourselves. You and I have to take the initiative to pursue something new. We are all resistant to change so we have to work hard to make it happen in our lives, particularly in this area of loving those who are different from us.

Differences aren't bad. Since we each bear the image of God, our differences help us see and understand God in deeper way. We miss God when we demand that our own culture be the center of life rather than part of the whole. The reason we all need change is that we naturally sink ourselves into our own cultural space, theological understanding, and socioeconomic class. These feel like safe places to many of us. Change then represents risk and venturing into the unknown. So we all need to hear some good stories of people who went through this kind of transformation—of what they experienced and how they came through with stronger relationships as a result.

Take a minute to think about some of the relationships in your life. What would happen if these people changed? Who are the people you'd be least comfortable with changing? How would you approach them if they changed? What if they started believing something you don't believe? And who are the people—both individuals and groups—that you consider the least reconcilable as they are currently? What if you were to just accept these people as they are without your expectations keeping you at a distance?

Such reconciliation is not impossible with God—it's the theme running through the entirety of Scripture and of history. God specializes in restoring relationships. The angels proclaimed that Christ's incarnation was all about peace on earth. And that peace (*shalom* in the Hebrew) is not just an absence of war or an end of hostilities but an all-encompassing flourishing in which individuals and communities grow into being all they were meant to be. By the grace of God and in the power of resurrection, our relationships can flourish.

Jesus told a story to illustrate what the kingdom of God is like. We usually call it the parable of the prodigal son. It resonates with us because we can see ourselves in the prodigal son, but the title is a bit misleading because it's really more about the father, who represents God. The father loved both the son who changed and the son who remained. Their relationships were different but remained intact all the same. This parable summarizes the reality of all of human history and how we relate as sons and daughters to God our Creator. God sees us coming from a distance or holds us close at home; either way, we're lavished with kisses and given a seat at the table by the one who loves us deeply.

The prime directive for Jesus' disciples is to take the power of the resurrection and be about the business of making that restoration real, in their lives and the lives of everyone else in the time and place in which they live. We are to work for reconciliation even in the hard places and with the hard people in our lives—including our enemies.

PRINCIPLES OF COMMUNICATION THAT FOSTERS HEALTHY CHANGE

In every good relationship, confrontation needs to happen. Confrontation shouldn't destroy the relationship but allow it to grow and deepen. But confrontation seems to be something that many people struggle with. It's difficult to confront the people we love, let alone the people we don't care too much for or don't know all that well. When we don't care for someone it's easy to justify not talking with them directly but talking about them with others. This leads to more hurt than anything else. Or we might go full-bore at someone and tell them exactly how we feel without much care for them or their feelings. This approach is dangerous—it can lead to violence and public embarrassment if it gets too far out of hand. The best way to confront a person is by taking the Scripture that asks us to speak the truth in love and to consider others better than ourselves seriously. Confrontation is not easy, but when done with love it can be a powerful tool to close gaps between people and to help relationships grow.

When engaging in conflict we also have to be careful to communicate clearly and well. This is difficult in the midst of tension, crosscultural engagement, or differing personality styles. We can say we communicated one thing while the other party took it in a completely different away. There's a saying about this: seek first to understand and then to be understood. Many of us do the opposite. We try to prove our point or let our bias inform our understanding before listening. When we think we already know the story, it can be a tragedy.

The Israelites thought they knew the Babylonians and God's plan for them, so they entered Babylon with bad attitudes and assumptions and songs about dashing the city's infants against the rocks. God told them to care for the city and plant gardens instead. Planting gardens of good crosscultural communication is a necessity for reconciliation. We live in a world where bias and judgment of the other is rampant. It leads to tensions on every level. From fighting in school yards to war between nations, the assumptions we make about one another lead ultimately to death. The graveyards literally and figuratively are full of broken relationships because we don't take the time to communicate well. This means listening first and speaking later.

Over the years I've discovered a number of principles required for our attempts to establish relationships across cultures. Each involves a bit of self-examination and intentional choice. Let me share four such principles:

1. My assumptions about other people are going to be challenged, and I need to be willing to get rid of my preconceptions and stereotypes. We have been inundated with all sorts of false labels, and we need to stop relating to people based on false assumptions.
2. My judgments about the way others live—their values, goals, and ways of doing things—must be suspended. I need to seek to understand, not to judge.
3. Creating community across cultures requires a whole lot of listening. We can't listen enough. We have to listen constantly to the people we are choosing to love. If we want to form good relationships, there's no way of getting around listening to strangers and the other in our lives.
4. Deep relationships require that we extend love and forgiveness, not just to close friends and family, but to each and every person. The individual family has its place, but we have overemphasized what this means to the exclusion of others in our lives.

Community requires us to commit to stay in relationships even when they're not comfortable. It means pushing ourselves to be comfortable with outsiders until they become trusted friends. It involves living through the awkward moments and misunderstandings and allowing them to move us deeper into relationship rather than using them as excuses to leave. Leaving a hard relationship has become easy in our society. We leave marriages, work, and even children. This is a major problem. We must learn how to commit through hardship if we are going to overcome our relational breakdowns. All relationships are hard. The difference between the good ones and the ones we leave comes down to our commitment and obedience: commitment to another person however they enter our lives and obedience to Christ in loving others better than ourselves.

We hinder relationships when we don't question our preconceived notions about people and who they are. Let people surprise you. Put your biases away and let people introduce themselves on their terms. Being open to someone different is a big step toward seeing relationships flourish. When we're not open to someone, we either try too hard and drive them away or we think we have them figured out before anything gets started. Both of these approaches need to soften a bit. Let's try to discern who the other is in the moment before us. Casting aside our ideas and prejudices and listening in the moment is a gift we can give to each other.

Race is a social construction based on privilege. Don't lead the relationship with your privilege—get to know people authentically on their terms. Introduce yourself, not with a title, position, or agenda, but as a person who is interested in getting to know another person. Our employment situation and titles (or lack of them) can become barriers to understanding each other. Our stereotypes play out in a big way when we look at people through the lens of our jobs. Some white people can jump. There are black people who camp. There are many Asian people who are outspoken. Even though these stereotypes may seem ridiculous when written down, many people still recite them.

Culture is central to our identity and criticizing it outside of relationships only leads to disconnection and breakdown with others. People don't like to be studied or objectified. There is beauty in our cultural diversity. Honoring is usually better than analyzing. And moving toward healthier relationships will only occur as we let go of our barriers and preconceptions and are willing to let our own hearts, minds, and souls be changed to fully embrace others.

5

GOING THE DISTANCE

Build houses and settle down; plant gardens and eat what they produce. Marry and have sons and daughters; find wives for your sons and give your daughters in marriage, so that they too may have sons and daughters. Increase in number there; do not decrease.

Jeremiah 29:5-6

This chapter is about living in hard places for the long haul. I recognize that not everyone is living in a hard place or is called to a hard place. There are many of you who love where you live and it's not difficult for you to be there. This chapter may be a stretch for some to identify with. But there are others who feel called to live in a different context or more diverse place. The lessons in this chapter help us recognize that there are difficult places to live. Perhaps knowing more about them will be helpful if you decide to live with or next to the other.

Dr. John Perkins is the founder of the Christian Community Development Association and a longtime advocate of civil rights whose writings and speaking has changed the landscape of how we think about serving in struggling neighborhoods. He says that if you aren't planning to stay in a place at least fifteen years you don't need to go. You need to stay long enough to establish deep relationships over time.

After getting married, Donna and I moved from our neighborhood in Southwest Philly to the other side of town into what we felt was a better neighborhood. But a few years later Donna and I were called to move back to Southwest Philly. This was not easy for me to wrap my head around since we had purposefully moved out of that neighborhood several years before. Here we were moving back into the same house I moved out of when we got married! It was clear this was where God wanted us to live, but that didn't make it easy. Embracing where you come from is a good thing, but it's not always the easiest thing to do.

Carlos lived across the street with his wife and two children. He was an incredible blessing to my life. We would leave for work at the same time each morning and return home close to same time. I spent many evenings just sitting outside talking and doing life with Carlos. It was good to have another brother my age living on our block, as challenging as that block could be at times. Carlos and I would often talk about those challenges—the challenges of living in a community where many couldn't afford to make ends meet, which led to struggles like drug trafficking and houses that needed repair. We lived in a food desert, so we had to drive or go a distance for groceries, and there were no banks, only predatory check cashing places. This often led to conversations of leaving the neighborhood. We loved our neighbors and each other, but many times the challenges seemed overwhelming. Carlos talked about moving and at times expressed the thought that Donna and I were crazy for not looking to move. Then one day Carlos announced that he and his family had purchased a home on the other side of town. I smiled and celebrated with him, but internally it hit me like a ton of bricks. Carlos's move brought up some things that had been brewing beneath the surface of my thoughts and feelings. I became very envious of Carlos and started to ask God why I had to stay in this neighborhood.

But had I really settled in my neighborhood? Carlos leaving opened questions about my commitment to it. Was I just waiting for my time in this old community to end and to be set free to leave? When I examined my heart, the answers to both were yes. I wasn't there for the long haul. But God wanted my commitment to be to this neighborhood and to my neighbors for as long as he deemed it necessary. He wasn't making any bargains or timelines.

If I were to have called the shots when Carlos left I would have left my neighborhood too. When things get hard, it's easy to justify moving away from the places where we are called, and the more privilege we have the easier those moves are to make. The hard things usually expose our level of commitment, and many times we find that our commitment has fallen short. We don't like hard things, and we avoid them at all costs because we have come to believe comfort is a major value in God's plan for us. But we should expect hardship. We should know that if we settle into places as a people who represent peace, common good, and the gospel, it is destined to be difficult. If we don't understand this, short commitments become the norm and we become a culture of short, easy, shallow obligations.

For much of our culture, short-term moves have come to be the norm. College students expect a four-year stay, graduate students as little as two. Missional engagements, internships, tours of military duty, business, and other opportunities are often designed as one-, two-, or three-year commitments. And these can all condition us to staying for short periods of time—to taking a short-term approach to the place where we live and to the relationships we have there. This mobility can provide us with varied experiences, the opportunity to see more of the world, to experience different cultures, and to add to the number of deep relationships in our lives. But often we can get through those different phases of our life journeys without putting down any roots or establishing any lasting friendships.

THREE APPROACHES TO LIVING IN BABYLON

When we find ourselves in Babylon, we have three basic options for how we can approach our time there. The first involves assuming that our stay will be a temporary one. This was the temptation for the Israelites. They hoped with all their hearts that the Lord would deliver them—soon—from the hard place where they found themselves. In their case, the Lord made it clear that such deliverance would not occur in their generation. But in our lives, the Lord may not always speak to us about the duration of our stay as clearly as he did to them. What if you knew the place where you are was going to be the only place for you and your children? I think we would live differently if we knew our grandchildren would live in some of the harder places we may be called or currently live.

We can choose to remain isolated from the community in which we've landed, refusing to have more to do with the hard people around us than we absolutely must. This is certainly what the Israelites would have wanted—after all, their new neighbors were Babylonians. The natural temptation would have been to remain aloof, to build walls and fences, to keep to themselves as much as possible. In our hard places we can disconnect and find coping mechanisms rather than seek out genuine relationships. We'll go other places to see friends, to relax, to be with people like us. This limits the possible depth of relationships right where we are. We wind up with a short stay or a long misery.

May I suggest that a short-stay approach is not really an option for those of us who are followers of Christ? I believe that even if we know with certainty that we'll be moving on after a year or two, our task is to make the most of the time we are given in all of the places to which we have been called. We are to be engaged with the world around us, and that applies to all of our lives, not just after we've arrived or retired or otherwise settled into the place we know that we'll be for the rest of our lives.

The second option is staying and hoping the culture around us will change. This option looks to change the people and their ways of life based on our own values, political choices, and opinions. This option is deadly. It constantly works to displace, move, and relocate current culture. We see this with gentrification.

The third option is to seek beloved community. It's a way of living that honors all people, works through difficulties with nonviolent negation, listens to current cultures and trends, and shares the resources of the community equitably. It works for good schools and parks for everyone and the creation of new spaces for diverse culture to flourish.

Donna and I ended up staying in that community for eight more years after Carlos moved. We participated with the block club and neighborhood association, helped keep our streets clean, and I even led a protest against our transportation system. We loved our neighbors and worked to establish justice for ourselves and the people living in our community

Christians have traditionally taken their marching orders from Jesus' words in Matthew 28:19-20, which begins, "Therefore go and make disciples . . ." The Greek word here translated as "go" could just as accurately be translated as "as you go." But we might overlook another important Scripture: "Love the Lord your God . . . and love your neighbor as yourself" (Mt 22:37-39). When you put the two of these together the difference in emphasis is this: We are all going somewhere every day, whether to class, to work, to ministry meetings, to the store, to the gym. *As we go* we are to be the hands and feet of Jesus. We should seek to be connected with and caring toward the people and places around us as a command of Jesus.

The decisions we make about place seem to hinge on questions like *Will I earn more money here?* and *Is this place comfortable?* as opposed to *Are the relationships I have here worth continuing even if it means less money and comfort?* The decision to live with less money and comfort seems a bit easier when we choose to stay with the people of that place and absolutely absurd when we would rather avoid those folks. The decision to pursue a place with the other in mind is perhaps one of the missing pieces of our faith: we may see a vibrant understanding of the other emerge as we make significant life choices based on the hard people in our lives. Can you imagine staying at a job simply because there's someone there you think God wants you to relate to (and who drives you nuts)? Can you imagine the depth of Christian life we can reach if loving the other meant giving over personal preferences as an offering in order to deepen relationships?

COMMITTING TO THE PLACE

The technology that has arisen in the last decade has made it easy for us to keep in constant contact with family and friends even when we're separated by miles or even oceans. But those same technologies can keep us from being present with the people who are physically nearby.

The 2009–2010 Georgia Tech men's basketball team was a promising collection of mostly younger players, some of whom were top recruits. But their regular season play was disappointing: although they had reached as high as fifteenth in the national rankings in week five, the Yellow Jackets ultimately fell out of the rankings altogether. During the weeklong Atlantic Coast Conference tournament, they finally came together, played to their potential, and made it to the championship game, where they narrowly fell to the (eventual national champion) Duke Blue Devils.

What made the difference? What is the explanation for the team's turnaround and their success during that critical playoff run? Well, an important factor may have been that coach Paul Hewitt took away his players' cell phones at the beginning of that week. For the first time, these guys were forced to be present with their teammates. Instead of being in constant text and phone communication with family and friends back home, they had the time to celebrate with, get to know, and bond with the other guys in the locker room, on the bus, and at meals. They were able to achieve their potential only after they made a commitment to establishing relationships with one another.

Our stay in Babylon may sometimes be short but we should commit to that community as though generations of our family will be there. We need to commit to loving that place and its people. It isn't really an option for us to just put in our time and not make a difference. We can't justify staying detached. Instead, we need to be ambassadors for Christ's kingdom for whatever timeframes God has us in those hard places.

We may also need to recognize that our situation has the potential of being long term. We might be in that hard place for a long, long time, and maybe even a lifetime. This was what the Israelites were forced to recognize through the message of the Lord's prophet Jeremiah. As with the Israelites of Jeremiah's day, I believe that the Lord calls his followers today to build and settle, to put down roots, and establish relationships for the Babylon to which he has taken us.

CULTIVATING YOUR COMMUNITY

The very first commandment God gave to human beings was to serve and protect the garden he had specially prepared for them. We were created to be good stewards of the bountiful and beautiful flora and fauna in this very good creation. And though a result of the fall was brokenness in our relationship with the rest of creation, the Creator did not rescind his command that his people be responsible for the stewardship of all that he had made. This also means stewarding our relationships with one another.

Christ's death on a Roman cross provided the way for redemption and healing to come to the broken relationship between God and humanity. But it was also intended to bring reconciliation between all of creation and the Creator (Col 1:15-20). And we, as those who have entered into the resurrection life of Christ, have been given the ministry of reconciliation (2 Cor 5:18-20) and are called to be stewards of the kingdom of God on earth.

The Israelites who were exiled in Babylon were commanded to plant gardens and eat produce from them. And although in our modern economy many of us are not dependent on food that we ourselves must grow, planting—whether vegetables or flowers or trees—remains one of the surest ways of committing ourselves to the place we are living in. Although I'm a city boy and not one to know much about planting, because I know and love the Creator I recognize that we have to surround ourselves with natural beauty, thereby bringing glory to him.

On the block where you live—what better way to embrace that place and neighborhood than to plant a young tree whose shade you won't be able to enjoy until several years later? This is one of the ways we can show the love of Christ: by beautifying grounds and leaving the space more attractive than when we arrived. We may even need to consider exactly what the Israelites were commanded to do—plant a garden and eat its produce. Could your neighbors benefit from a community garden, and might you be the one to initiate that?

The instruction to plant and eat was also a way for God to let the Israelites know that they needed to sustain themselves in Babylon. It was a commitment to work and to wait for that work to produce benefits. It was an investment in the economy of Babylon through work that sustained them and others around them. Perhaps the gardens you spend time on are the relationships with the people around you. Take time to water those relationships every day, till the hard ground with confrontation, and pick out the weeds of miscommunication. This kind of relational work doesn't show fruit overnight.

GREEN MY HOOD

Urban neighborhoods are dangerous places, environmentally speaking. Trash dumps, tow lots, expressways, and chemical plants create situations that are unsafe. Being a good neighbor today means more than just planting a garden and eating its produce. Is it possible to create a new economy in the hood that would generate jobs, lower energy costs, reduce the carbon footprint of an urban neighborhood, and allow neighbors to get to know one another at the same time? I think there just might be a way to make this a reality.

Our urban neighborhoods can begin to help themselves and lower their risks by starting their own green projects. We can train and hire people to do audits in homes that are full of lead paint, leaky windows, clogged gutters, and uninsulated water heaters. This training would create jobs and lower energy bills for residents, as well as reduce a neighborhood's negative impact on God's creation.

We can grow neighborhood gardens and establish farmers' markets, which would offer neighbors better access to nutritious foods that are otherwise very costly and unavailable at inner-city food stores and in food deserts. We can make neighborhoods safer for walking, so that neighbors can get around without driving. That means less asthma-causing air pollution, fewer emergency room visits, and fewer sleepless nights for worried parents.

Caring for the environment has hit the hood and is now a major urban issue, and people of faith have the opportunity to offer new ways to do this. This is no longer just an issue of global warming and saving rain forests—it is about protecting some of our most vulnerable citizens. Through green job training, youth receive job skills, financial resources, and greater responsibility in their communities. Neighbors benefit from reduced energy costs, cleaner indoor and outdoor environments, and improved health. And entire communities grow in health, safety, and dignity. Jeremiah's words about Babylon apply today to your own neighborhood: "In its welfare you will find your welfare."

The dream of greening my hood is becoming a reality through the church's obedience to God's will. Green job-training programs already exist throughout the country, bringing work to thousands of youth and millions of dollars of savings to urban communities. Some of these programs should to be rooted in the church so that this good stewardship is infused with the deeper hope of Christ's love. Following Jesus' command to clothe the naked, care for the sick, and feed the hungry now means, in part, providing clean air, safe streets, and healthy neighborhoods for our poor urban neighbors. Churches are ideally positioned to provide hope in environmentally dangerous neighborhoods and economically frightening times by doing just what Jesus asked of us.

The idea of planting gardens in Babylon means creating an economy that produces work while sustaining ourselves. Conversely, the call to sustain ourselves in hard places means creating ways for others to thrive. Israel's call to plant gardens in Babylon is a community development model, and it models God's call for us to find ways for our neighbors to thrive in the midst of our personal planting and harvesting. We don't just plant and harvest for ourselves but for the community at large. We need to develop systems that cause prosperity for all.

One of the ways we realized this in my neighborhood in Atlanta were tire cleanup days. It seems that some people saw our neighborhood as a dumping ground. We found and discarded hundreds of tires that had been illegally dumped in our neighborhood. Local neighbors who took responsibility for cleaning them up were not only greening their neighborhood but properly disposing of dangerous materials from around the city in the form of old tires.

When many suburban neighbors drive into our cities to work each day, the amount of pollution affects urban neighbors, many of whom live with disproportionately less income. The people who are driving less and making use of public transportation (which is better for the environment) are suffering the ills of their suburban neighbors who are polluting the air more. Suburbanites taking the bus or train regularly would help us all. In this way, embracing the other may simply look like a public commute.

SETTLING IN FOR THE LONG HAUL

I've spent many years in ministry watching and counseling people on how to build and settle into new places, specifically, places that are culturally different. Many times a breakdown occurs in the establishment of long-term commitment.

Settling in for the long haul involves establishing residency and making certain changes that project a sense of permanency. You change your driver's license and your car's registration. You register to vote in a new state, city, and precinct. You haven't really settled in to that new place—emotionally or in practical terms—until you've done these sorts of things. And doing these things makes a difference in your ability to build friendships.

While settling in and making commitments to a new place, we should take the option of looking for people, groups, and places where we can invest time and energy to go deeper. The people already in that place will likely be more willing to reciprocate, since we have made an effort that suggests our commitment for the long haul. This can be one of the more challenging hurdles to crosscultural engagement, because living a life among people who are different means we risk misunderstanding people and being misunderstood. We may also experience loneliness as we try to establish our sense of place.

Settling into a place for the long haul takes discipline, especially if it calls for significant crosscultural engagement. Becoming established in a new place may call for things like learning a new language or changing eating habits. And while a language difference is an obvious potential barrier, differences in culture and values can be both less obvious and more problematic. Such differences require us to listen, learn, seek to understand, and submit to others who may be quite different from those we've been familiar with and comfortable with in the past.

Settling into a new culture takes time, and it takes a commitment to not walk away when things get hard. The dedication to stay at the table is vital if we are ever going to settle into relationship with a culture and community that is not our native one. The freedom to walk away from crosscultural relations can be catastrophic. It can convey to the other people involved that the relationship is not worth our effort, or that it will work only under our own terms. Demanding our own terms limits depth to relationships, and, of course, where there is no depth, it becomes easy to walk away when (not *if*) difficult times come. The result—played out over and over again across our nation and world—is devastating to the people involved and heartbreaking for our society as a whole. When we settle into a place, common needs, and shared experiences create the relational mortar that can hold together what's been built when storms come to rage against it.

The irony here is that the things that sustain us in hard places are the things that are the most difficult to figure out. When we're surrounded by strangers in a strange place, how do we find, get to know, and love people that will be willing to walk with us through our journey? How do we in community pursue God together when we come from different places?

We were made for community, but we are fallen, highly influenced by evil, and essentially selfish. We want our own way. I'm not sure when it happens, but somewhere during childhood we go from a disposition of sharing to a profound selfishness, and we have to be taught again not to be selfish. At one point, my children wanted to share everything. They would take a bite of something and then give it me, and though they had slobbered on it and I didn't want to eat it, I sometimes did because, well, they were sharing. But they eventually moved on to refusing to share, and we had to teach them how to share over and over again.

It's not so different as adults. We need to figure out when and what to share, and we need to acknowledge that to commit to long-term relationship means a call for a significant amount of sharing. This applies to commitments like marriage, business, and all sorts of community, and each of these relationships is difficult or impossible when we put ourselves first.

INTERRACIAL AND CROSSCULTURAL MARRIAGE

When you build and settle into a place where you think you are better than the people who live around you, there is a constant barrier to relationships. Authenticity can never emerge from a "better than" disposition.

There are very few markers in life that show how you feel about people and other groups better than marriage. Who my daughter or son marries is a measure like no other.

Interracial marriage wasn't completely legalized until 1967. The fact that it was considered a problem showcases our deep racial problem. I think we can learn from families that are multicultural—not that they have all the answers, but because it's an overlooked place. There is something about becoming family that is challenging and an even deeper challenge when it is between people of different races. My friend Sarah Quezada has great insights to share about her life and family with her husband, Billy, that I think can help us.

Multiracial Marital Hurdles by Sarah Quezada

People say marriage is hard. And some people say crosscultural friendships are hard. And then some of us are like, "Ooh, let's mash those together and see what we get. Sounds fun!" I am white. Born and raised in Tennessee and Kentucky, I'm Southern before I'm American. And I met my Guatemalan, now-husband at a multicultural church plant in Los Angeles.

He is a Guatemalan descendant of light-skinned Spanish immigrants (or conquistadors, you might say) to Central America. He identifies fully as Guatemalan in the same way I claim the United States rather than my historical German ancestry. But perhaps the unexpected confusion others express around his ethnic background mirrors some of the ambiguity we experience as a crosscultural couple. We don't clearly fit standard categories and expectations, and this is both a painful surprise and an unexpected gift. The feeling of not fitting in has been a reality in our marriage. We both were living crosscultural lifestyles before we met, but marriage is a lifelong commitment to never quite being at home in your culture ever again. Even the rhythms and traditions that stir up warm memories in our hearts or evoke sentiments of "home" can make us feel disconnected from each other. I will need to remind my husband that Thanksgiving is "a thing," and yes, I will feel emotional if we make no plans and just stay at home eating frozen pizza. And at Christmastime, we will eat tamales on Nochebuena and open stockings Christmas morning so that both of us experience the joy of passing our traditions on to our kids. We are intentional about participating in the cultural rituals that are important and meaningful to the other. But we cannot always fully understand or relate.

Not quite fitting in has unlocked surprises that I never saw coming. It has drawn me closer to God in new ways. We're warned not to get too comfortable in our culture and that this world is not our home. Crosscultural marriage has helped me shed some of my comfort in my culture. I cannot fully submerge any longer because I am bound to someone who cannot join me fully in my culture. I also find I am drawn to Jesus, who is both fully God and fully man. Who can understand that bicultural concept better than my kids, who are fully Guatemalan and fully Georgian? Jesus engaged the traditions of his Jewish culture but also turned them on end. When I experience cultural loneliness, I am comforted by a God who never truly fit in and felt connected to multiple worlds simultaneously. My crosscultural marriage has helped me relate to this tension I see in the Bible, and it has nurtured a new thanksgiving for the Christ child who so deeply understands our crosscultural experience.

BRINGING THE KINGDOM

When we find ourselves in a hard place and have determined by God's grace to seek deep community and long-lasting relationships there, then we may be able to make some commitments—commitments that are so real and risky that if carried out we set ourselves up to solve problems in a whole new way. Commitments like embracing the hard place enough to raise our kids there and trusting God enough to care for them. We model for our children and grandchildren a world of dignity for all people. Those interactions become a beacon of hope to all people. Our goal is to see our own descendants live in a better world because of the relationships we have forged in difficult times and places.

Our attitudes and behaviors—in this tough place and among these difficult people—are helping to bring the kingdom of heaven to this corner of the earth, for the sake of future generations and to the glory of our Lord. Embrace your community, settle in for the long haul, and see how the Lord uses you to help your neighborhood flourish.

6

TAKE ME OUT TO THE BALL GAME

Tradition, which is always old, is at the same time ever new because it is always reviving—born again in each new generation, to be lived and applied in a new and particular way.

Thomas Merton, *No Man Is an Island*

We walked into Philly's Veterans Stadium. The ramps were long and my excitement grew more and more as we ascended higher and higher. I was there to see the Phillies after having watched so many games on television. I ran with my brothers and cousins up the ramps. My uncle kept trying with no success to calm us down. Five boys, gloves in hand, at their first game; calm was not on the agenda. When we stepped out it was a sight to behold. The lights, the field, the green manicured grass, the large scoreboard, the players warming up that seemed so close (and the hot dogs, of course). I fell in love with baseball that night. I love baseball to this day. I don't know if my uncle knew I would fall in love with the game then but in that moment a tradition was born. My uncle successfully passed on his love of the game to me by getting me close to it and letting the game come alive in me.

TRADITION AND CHANGE

As believers, we often act as though our identity with the church and its tradition is some dry, stale expression of something old that can't be passed on and renewed. Our lack of deep, dynamic relationships with one another and a genuine love for God has marred our experience of Christian tradition with artificial rules and shallowness. But we have the opportunity, as the world gets more and more diverse, to apply an old tradition to a new era. This tradition understands that God has made each of us in his image and that we are called to honor the *imago Dei* in each person. This tradition invites all of creation to be known and accepted. This tradition is not stagnant or boring; it's life itself and it should be renewed in each generation. It's about how we love the other. It's about the acceptance of all people. We have forgotten how to introduce people to this game, this tradition, but we can pass it on through highlighting new ways forward into a better world.

Latasha Morrison has begun a community called "Be the Bridge" to Racial Unity, which was launched at the 2015 IF: Gathering conference for women. It's creating new spaces for conversations on race with the hope of a better world emerging. Each group offers space for dialogue as a diverse collection of people, and they challenge problems of race and culture together. This new expression of tradition doesn't throw out the old tradition; it only builds on it and offers a new way to relate through social networking.

We don't have to start the healing journey with giant steps. We can move forward by establishing simple traditions like a weekly coffee time or breakfast with someone. The small things are a bridge to something deeper. (How do you eat an elephant? One bite at a time.) Let's try to make small strides toward a common goal. Even if the goal is large, we can make small amounts of progress until the problem is conquered.

OPENING OUR SACRED SPACES

It's when we share our special places and things with each other that we can begin to know each other more deeply. I learned a lot about my uncle at the Phillies game. He wasn't worried about how loud we were; he hugged us and cheered with us, and he smiled and laughed more in that baseball game than I had seen him any other time. Veterans Stadium was his sacred place and he brought us into it and shared himself with us. We too can invite people into our sacred spaces, wherever they may be, and allow ourselves to be more fully known. Sacred spaces are where we relax, laugh, celebrate, and hug. They are inviting spaces where our humanity is on display. These are the places where we don't judge but welcome and where we don't separate but include.

Open your space and listen to someone else's story. Visit someone's sacred space and invite someone different into yours. We'll get to know each other in a new way. When we open our sacred space to the other in our lives we create new possibilities—new traditions that challenge the status quo and allow us to reimagine ourselves and our world.

To some, sacred spaces may seem like small things. I remember when we lived in Eastlake, a community in Atlanta. Groups often came to our neighborhood to clean up or paint something.

A group one Saturday came to the top of our block in a school bus. Forty or fifty white people piled out with trash bags and paint. The ones with trash bags started picking up trash and the others with the paint went to a wall that to them looked like a wall full of graffiti that needed to be painted. They began preparing their paint when one of the boys from the neighborhood, Jermaine, went and stood between them and the wall and let them know in no uncertain terms that they weren't going to touch that wall. The group was terrified and confused when I arrived there on the corner. I didn't know the group that had come, but I knew that the wall was sacred. It was where neighborhood guys would put the names of people killed in our neighborhood. It wasn't a frivolous wall of graffiti as one leader of the group had described. It was a memorial. We have to be careful of others' sacred places even when we don't understand them.

What followed that tense event was pretty cool. The next week a couple of the leaders of that group came down after tensions had died down and Jermaine consented to walk them through all the names on the wall. It was incredibly moving as he explained and lamented his friends. That day, the group leaders got to know who Jermaine is there in his sacred space. They saw his humanity and understood.

Donna loves to watch *Scandal* and have a glass of wine and some popcorn on Thursday evenings. It's a sacred space for her. I could take or leave *Scandal*, but she has invited me into that space and on Thursdays I enter into it with her for a few hours. Our relationship is way more important than my TV preferences. I don't prefer *Scandal* but I do prefer her, and if this is a space she sets aside and invites me into, I try my best to treat it with respect. Our relationship only grows deeper when I embrace her through honoring her space (whether it's sacred to me or not).

What are your sacred spaces? Is there a special television show that is your weekly getaway? Does listening to a certain type of music take your mind somewhere meaningful? Perhaps there are regular activities that have particular importance for you, like going hiking or taking long road trips. Maybe you have regular family gatherings or neighborhood events. Reading books? Bring someone different into these places and allow yourself to dream and start new traditions with other people. In my opinion, this is what will move us toward solving our problems differently. We open the door to deeper conversations and a deeper understanding of the other when our traditions routinely include them.

I hope we can learn to apply this sacred space principle to race. It's a large question for the world in which we live. Can we honor sacred space of the other by starting small and moving deeper one step at a time? Weekly activities, such as attending church, should move us into deeper issues.

MEMORIES THAT DEEPEN COMMUNITY

Throughout God's dealings with his people, he instituted traditions and practices meant to remind them of their standing as his children. The *Shema* of Deuteronomy 6 became the central grounding document—part of the mission statement—for the Israelites for most of their history. The practices prescribed in it were intended to keep them centered on their Creator-Redeemer even in the hard places like Babylon and during times of drought and desert.

In Joshua 4, as part of the account of the crossing of the Jordan into the Promised Land, we read of the Lord's instructions for one person from each of the twelve tribes to go back to the middle of the Jordan to retrieve a large stone. They were then to place these twelve stones in a pile as a memorial of God's miraculous deliverance. They were told that this cairn would serve as a reminder and as a teaching moment for generations to come. The children and grandchildren who did not personally experience the flight from Egypt, the parting of the Red Sea, the provision through years of wandering in the desert, and the crossing of the Jordan River would learn of those events—and of the powerful and caring God who brought them about—by asking about this standing pile of river rocks.

Jesus instituted two particular practices for us that serve, in part, as the memorial stones did for the Israelites: baptism and communion. They commemorate and reenact the central events in all of human and cosmic history, the death and resurrection of Jesus Christ. Baptism and communion unite us not only with the brothers and sisters gathered with us but with other Christians throughout the ages. They remind us of our miraculous deliverance from sin and death, and help to establish our identities as sons and daughters of God wherever we find ourselves living.

The Old Testament people of God had mixed success at remembering their God and at remaining unspoiled from the world. They frequently struggled with falling into the idolatrous and immoral practices of the pagan nations around them, and they often forgot their God and their identity as his chosen people. In our times, there is likewise a danger that we would become just like the world around us so we need to remain set apart from ungodly world influences. But this keeps many of us from engaging the world for fear that it will drag us down. I believe we need to creatively engage society with practices and traditions—like baptism, communion, and others—that distinguish us as those who have been redeemed by the Lord without fear but with joy, life, and sacrifice in ways that are inviting.

I would like to propose that the pagan principle we have let ruin us is our relationship with race and racism. Our greatest danger as a church and as believers is that we don't actually see all people as made in the image of God. This is an immoral practice and it has ruined how people view Christians in the world. That Sunday mornings are segregated is no big secret; we're heard it over and over. For the most part, our actions don't seem to be changing. Worship and its lack of diversity is a joke. What kind of God are we representing? I don't think we really care that we are segregated. We can quote Scriptures of love and grace and yet be as divided as we are—this is the influence of Babylon on the people of God, not the people of God influencing Babylon.

LET YOUR PASSION DRIVE YOUR TRADITIONS

Each spring, my son Jon and I set our calendars and get our baseball hats, jerseys, and jackets and travel to Florida for baseball's spring training. We don't do this alone: there are two other dads and their sons with us, and it's a tradition that's five years old now. Jon connects with those two other boys each year in Florida, and when they meet, they pick up right where they left off the year before. The boys are ten years old, and for half of their lives they've been going on this baseball trip. We actually get very little baseball in—the boys get pretty bored after about the fourth inning (we're hoping that gets better as they get older). So the boys hit the pool and carry on laughing and playing together. The record is twelve hours in the pool on one trip! Jon and the other boys are of different races and have very different family backgrounds, but this tradition links them in profound ways to each other and to their dads. The commitment from the beginning was baseball and our boys, but it has come to represent a meaningful tradition that has changed their lives. This tradition will help these three boys to see the world differently because of the common passions we've shared with each other.

Speaking of passions, I'm a football fan. I'm not a casual fan; I'm a bit over the top about my team and the game. I like to watch the pregame, the game itself, the postgame, and the recap and analysis. (I might have a problem, but that's for another book.) Super Bowl Sunday is a major holiday for me and it serves as one of the ways that our family has been able to start traditions within our community.

The moment the teams are set for the Super Bowl, I send out invitations to folks letting them know that the party around the game will be incredible. We decorate the entire house, we set up multiple TVs for varying levels of fans (casual fans who want to talk, fans who want to sit outside around a fire with blankets, teen fans, children, and then very serious fans with little chatter that's not related to football). There's food, outdoor grilling, halftime play for kids, prizes for picking the correct score, and voting for best commercial. All of this happens in our house and is open to the entire community and friends. This has been a tradition for the past thirty years of Donna and my married life. This tradition went on for many years in Philly, then in Atlanta, and now it carries on in Portland. Friends that know us know of our Super Bowl parties. This tradition has brought us together with many people across race, culture, and socioeconomic levels.

This is one of the ways my family and I have been able to break barriers. Barriers are walls we have set up culturally, some for good reasons, others out of preference, and whatever the reason, they are hard to penetrate. You might think that small parties and weekends watching baseball are minor but they are not—they are the sacred spaces we protect. But we are seeking to add depth to our relationships so that they can last over time and through storms, and this depth only comes after we move beyond our cultural barriers. When we let someone through our holiday-gathering, sports-watching, beer-drinking, book-club-reading, child's-birthday, happy-hour barriers we start to humanize the other. If we can get to humanization we can reach God. Reconciliation has everything to do with how we get to God together. If we can reach God together we have a shot at shalom.

THE NEW TESTAMENT PLOT TWIST

The idea and promise that God would use chosen people to bring blessing to all the nations can be traced all the way back to Abraham and Genesis 12. But for most of the Old Testament, it seemed like the most important goal for God's people was to keep apart from other people. This apparently was because their ability to remain morally and spiritually pure was easily compromised by their interaction with other cultures.

By the time Jesus—the long-awaited Messiah—came onto the scene, the Jews had implemented an entire system of rules that created a barrier between themselves and the various cultures around them. In the Jewish mind (and particularly that of the Pharisees), everyone who was not a Jew was outside of God's blessing and care. Each people group—Roman, Greek, barbarian, Samaritan—was pigeonholed and held in contempt, and to the extent possible, a good Jew would avoid all interaction with them.

Jesus cleared all of this up. Jesus fulfilled the promise of Genesis 12 and changed the focus for God's people from separation from the world to active engagement with it. Jesus modeled loving and serving the despised other, demonstrating that the kingdom is for all people.

The Jews of Jesus' day had no dealings with Samaritans; they were considered half breeds and not worthy to enter the sacred space of the temple with the "true" Israelites. But Jesus purposefully went through Samaria, a region where as Jew he was not supposed to go. There he spent time with a Samaritan—a Samaritan woman at that, and one who had been with four different husbands. Jesus invited her into his sacred space of worship, and she invited others there, which caused Jesus to remain even longer with them in that awkward and forbidden region. You see, Samaria was one of the hoods of the day and wasn't seen as a place where any significant relationships would occur. It was to be avoided at all costs. But Jesus entered this city and talked to this woman and these people as an example for us to follow. He stayed there longer and created stories and memories that I'm sure were told by those people from that time forward. This is clearly a reminder for us to go to places and connect with people we are told to avoid. A continued avoidance of the other over time will cause us to lack tradition crossculturally. The lack of tradition and story together is killing us all around the world. We must go through Samaria! We must go to others' ballgames.

Jesus told a parable about a wedding. Those who were invited to the wedding didn't respond, so the host opened the invitation up to all who wanted to be part of the party.

It's interesting that Jesus used a cultural setting to talk about the kingdom. Weddings are as cultural as you can get. I have performed many weddings and the beauty of them (in addition to the bride, of course) is their cultural distinctives.

I've performed weddings in small churches attended only by family and friends, weddings on the beach, a wedding in a large, steepled church where the bride had a train as long as the aisle. I did a wedding where I stepped on a glass, one where I jumped over a broom, and even one where I was barefoot. Each of these said something about the culture that the bride or groom had come from or wanted to establish. When you go to a wedding, you're expected to honor that couple's or that family's culture.

Our cultures are meant to be shared and not as ways to create exclusivity. As with a good wedding, we should celebrate the joining of families and cultures. Weddings aren't a place to judge, condemn, or study. Weddings are meant to celebrate the coming together and the hope of what will happen from this couple's union. We don't enter the wedding skeptical; we enter hopeful. This too is the way of the kingdom and the rejection of the pagan ways of exclusivity, racism, elitism, and sexism.

As products of their Jewish isolationism, Jesus' closest disciples had trouble getting the message of the inclusiveness of his kingdom. Though they were told to go into Judea, and Samaria, and to the uttermost parts of the earth, the early church did their best to remain together in Jerusalem until persecution eventually caused them to scatter. The church grew in the scattering, but even then it took them a while to share the good news with those outside the Jewish communities where they were scattered. The command was to go into Samaria and Jesus had modeled how we're to go, not as people with a holy chip on our shoulder, but as people who will encounter brothers and sisters at the well of life. We'll ask for a drink and we'll share stories with each other. There the gospel message emerges.

Peter finally got it, but only after he was given a vision and an angel intervened to connect him with a Roman centurion. Peter summed up his experience this way: "I now realize how true it is that God does not show favoritism but accepts from every nation the one who fears him and does what is right." For the apostle Paul, this expansion of God's blessing to include not just the Jews, but all people, was the great mystery hidden through the ages.

Today Christ's followers are called by him to go into every town and city—even the hard places—to join in the good news of his inbreaking kingdom. We are called to be a light and join with those who are witnesses in tough places. We are expected *not* to hide our light under a bushel, which means that we can't keep to ourselves in a holy huddle to ensure to keep away from evil influences.

TRADITIONS AND PRACTICES FOR THE KINGDOM

So can we create traditions and practices that are both kingdom focused *and* inclusive? Are there practices that we—as followers of Christ—might do to include our brothers and sisters that happen to look, talk, act, and worship differently than we do? Can we establish traditions that might bless those around us who are not followers of Christ, practices that might help us get to know our neighbors and other members of our communities? Can we be intentional about creating opportunities for just being friends with the folks around us, even if they are not the people we would have chosen or the place isn't where we'd really like to be?

I can't dictate what your practices and traditions ought to be (though I can share with you a couple of mine). Your context—your neighborhood, your hard place—is unique and will warrant unique traditions and practices. But the goals and objectives transcend contexts. We ought to be about tearing down barriers and creating pockets of understanding and love wherever we are. This includes bringing the good news of Christ's kingdom to those not experiencing it. But it also includes just being fully human, which in turn means doing a much better job of relating to other humans despite their differences.

Church does not outrank our identity with humanity. That's an evil idea. Have we ever failed to do a required act of generosity or meet an urgent need because we were waiting for our church to build a program around it? How many times have we helped our church set up a table or booth as our way of participating in a community or neighborhood event when what was really needed was for some of us Christians to help organize the event itself? As you think and pray about what practices and traditions you can use to create better understanding and community in your place, let me share one of mine.

There is a group of guys I have grown to love in Chicago. We're from different places and have various backgrounds. We started meeting whenever we can—when I visit Chicago or we otherwise find ourselves in the same place. The tradition is set around food and sharing our struggles as black men. It was started innocently enough as a Wednesday night gathering in Chicago and has grown into a deeper fellowship with each other. We don't see each other all that often, but five minutes in and it's like we see each other every day. These guys let me into their space and our relationship is solidified.

INCLUSIVE COMMUNITY

If we don't establish regular practices with others, we won't have rhythm in hard places—rhythms that can discipline us and allow us to be ourselves in safe space. Trust can be built through tradition. And when things become familiar through tradition, we often let our guard down and open up to relationship.

When you sit around the table or in a circle on the floor (depending on your family tradition), who is in the room? Who is special enough for you in that space that they can be included in a sacred tradition with you and your loved ones? With whom can you tell stories of the past and share fond memories? Have you allowed—or will you allow—those special spaces to be open to the difficult other in your life? Are you willing to create memories with people or in places that you don't know well? Are you willing to chart new territory or create a totally new sacred space with different people?

Thanksgiving is my favorite holiday, and for years it was celebrated with family and close friends in Philly. It meant sitting around the football game, talking loud, screaming at the TV, and eating good food. When Donna and I had children, we began adding lights up on the house that evening to bring in the Christmas season. When we moved to Atlanta we couldn't always afford to go back to Philly for Thanksgiving, so we had to rely on the community around us, which was more diverse than my community in Philly. We started inviting others over and having them bring small things for the dinner. It quickly became a tradition. Our new community would gather together with new family members and traditions combined with ours. It made way for some great memories.

A couple in our church in Atlanta started the turkey trot, where every Thanksgiving we would get up and do a walk/run with people from all ages, races, and Thanksgiving traditions. It was a new Thanksgiving tradition and it went on and continues in small ways even today. It was our way of celebrating in a new place that brought life, laughter, and tradition.

I can't help but think that the gospel itself calls us to be open with our sacred spaces and to constantly be willing to let others join in our traditions. The table is always open and changing as new people enter the kingdom, thereby changing the space over and over. The practice of hospitality and the Communion table suggest that others are always welcome in our sacred and safe space. This may be why we are instructed to check our hearts as we enter the Communion space and make things up with our sister or brother. Some of the sisters and brothers with us at the Communion table may be people who we wouldn't normally welcome into our sacred spaces because of our barriers based on race, gender, or socioeconomic status.

It seems to me that the church is the perfect place to create new traditions. Church is a place that can be welcoming to all people and open to relationships. I want to believe that the cross can be a rallying point for creating new spaces. The disciples, especially Peter, were challenged to move into the new, and the new was dinner with Cornelius. Take the old, learn from it, keep the sacred space, but add new people to it! The disciples had their problems trying to figure things out but eventually the new began to speak and offer hope. We too can offer hope as we yield to the new in our lives. Many times we try to protect the past and our usual ways instead of welcoming the new. Our fear drives us instead of our trust in God and people. But fear is not our friend; it is indeed our enemy and one I hope we learn to chase away.

New traditions help people create memories and experiences together that will shape their collective stories. Traditions can be as simple as a meal or as complex as a trip taken each year; either way, they allow us to share in relationships and to reminisce. We must create traditions that cause us to reminisce together across race and cultural lines. These recollections stay with us, and when difficult times arise, the good we know of one another—the time spent, the tears shed, the misunderstandings—serves as the material that allows us to be human together. When someone is human to us, we respond differently. Grace seems to find its way into our relationships when we share a common memory.

Our Christian practices in the midst of hard places become the glue between us, allowing us to know each other deeply. We are commanded to love deeply—not lightly or only when things are good. Loving deeply is when we love people through hard times and disappointments. The depth of our love kicks in when we are able to forgive our sisters and brothers even when it's not deserved. Jesus' love was shown for us while we were sinners. Love and forgiveness create friends in a way that nothing else does. Friendship is where tradition lives and thrives. We are able to establish long-term traditions because our love goes deep.

Deep love abides, meaning it stays and walks through spaces that are not easy or deserving—the friend you have to walk through an addiction with or the spouse you forgive of adultery. These are examples of love covering sin, stepping into someone's life and offering something they need and not necessarily what they deserve. The traditions and life practices that emerge from this type of love last a lifetime and help us embrace the diversity of those who God has called us to love.

7

NATURAL JUSTICE

Seek the peace and prosperity of the city to which I have carried you into exile. Pray to the LORD *for it, because if it prospers, you too will prosper.*

Jeremiah 29:7

When my family and I moved to South Atlanta in 2000, there was a local park about a block from our house. The first week we lived there I walked up to the park with Jess, Josh, and Joel. The basketball court was full of glass and trash and there were no rims, just backboards. My daughter has loved basketball since she was five years old and wanted to play, so I had to find a way to get those courts operating. I called the city first and got nothing but the runaround. It was my daughter who wanted to play ball and in my anger with the city and their lack of cooperation, I decided to do something myself. I got a ladder, brooms, and a blower and went up to the courts to sweep them off, blow the leaves away, and replace the rims and nets. I did this so that my daughter could play. Fixing and cleaning those courts gave not only my daughter a place to play ball but now every kid in the neighborhood could play. Caring for my kids became a natural work of justice for all kids. Now every family could benefit from what was done. This justice was natural and not an act of service or an event. It was planted into the rhythm of my life and relationships. Of course I should have been interested in fixing that court even if it weren't just about my daughter, but I was much more likely to fix it because of the relationship I have with my daughter. I wanted to support her and in doing so I supported every kid in the community.

The Israelites of Jeremiah's day were expected to work and pray for the welfare of the foreign city to which they'd been carried. I imagine they found what the Lord was asking of them to be a difficult thing. The Babylonians whose welfare they were to seek were not only of a different nation, a different ethnicity, and a different religion—they were the avowed enemies of God's people. God seems to have cared an awful lot about the welfare of all people—about peace and justice for all—to make such demands of his people during their exile.

Justice is not something that God does. He *is* just. Justice cannot be separated out from the nature of God. There is no justice without him. It's like trying to separate love from his nature. Where there is love, there is God, and where there is justice, there is God. It's a natural outpouring of his very being. This can more difficult for us when we think about justice in terms of people we don't know or care for very much. We want justice for ourselves and those close to us but perhaps not for those we don't care as much to know. Justice for loved ones can easily override our sense of justice for our enemies.

I suspect that God cares just as much today as he did in Jeremiah's time about human flourishing, about peace and justice for all. And allow me to suggest that we in twenty-first-century America still struggle mightily with achieving peace and justice in the cities in which we live. Sure, some of our neighbors have a different a skin color, different religious views, belong to a different political party, or live in a different socioeconomic sphere. But by and large we're talking about fellow Americans, and the fact of the matter is, we just can't seem to get along.

Recent events in Florida, Ferguson, North Charleston, Ohio, South Carolina, and Baltimore are only the most obvious and better-documented examples that our own cities are not characterized by peace and justice. These events are stark reminders that we need to continue to seek the justice of others who may be different than we are. I believe that Christ is calling us, his people, to lead in seeking peace and justice today. What's more, I believe that by the very same power that raised Jesus from the dead we can expect to achieve the welfare, peace, and justice that he intended for our cities, nation, and world. Shalom is possible. But achieving shalom is very difficult work that must be rooted in relationships. This can be achieved in a more natural way when we have shared life and space. Justice for all is a common goal realized out of connection with others.

We all seek justice for ourselves and for those close to us. If our kid gets murdered we want justice. If our close family is mistreated we want justice. It's natural. *Natural* meaning we accept it as a regular part of life. We fight for what we believe is right. This is embedded in us from our Creator whose nature is just. I don't think we can help ourselves about justice—we scream for it. But this sense of justice breaks down when we don't seek it for those who are different from us; most of the time, we don't scream for justice for those we don't know. We may speak out or say something if it's convenient, but the passionate call and desire for what's right is reserved for our close relationships. The more connection we feel to someone who is treated unjustly, the stronger our appeal for justice. We fight for our friends. We fight for people we can relate to. But we should be fighting for all.

In the book of Amos, the prophet writes, "But let justice roll on like a river, righteousness like a never-failing stream!" (Amos 5:24). Amos cries for justice and initiates a call to everyone to remember who God is—that he demands and expects justice for all, especially for the poor. We have sectioned off justice for our friends and those we like, but have forgotten God wants it for everyone. A lack of justice for all people shows itself more intensely among the poor and marginalized. This sentiment is repeated by Dr. King in his "Letter from Birmingham Jail" in which he challenges religious leaders in the South:

> Any law that degrades human personality is unjust. All segregation statutes are unjust because segregation distorts the soul and damages the personality. It gives the segregator a false sense of superiority and the segregated a false sense of inferiority. To use the words of Martin Buber, the great Jewish philosopher, segregation substitutes an "I-it" relationship for the "I-thou" relationship, and ends up relegating persons to the status of things.

WALLS DON'T CREATE PEACE

In Belfast, Northern Ireland, and its surrounding area, there is a series of so-called peace walls that separate neighborhoods that don't get along with one another. They were erected to stem the violent conflicts that have for decades taken place between two different people groups. Largely of the same ethnicity, these people are divided by religion (Protestant Christians and Roman

Catholic Christians) and politics (Unionists who want to remain within the United Kingdom and Nationalists who would rather become part of the Irish Republic).

Some of Northern Ireland's peace walls were built in 1969, and they have now far outlasted the Berlin Wall. They have been largely successful at stemming the violence that used to rage between close neighbors with different religious and political affinities. But tension persists to this day between the people living in these separated communities. They express fear, distrust, and hatred of the people living just across the fence. Most spend their entire lives without getting to meet or know their nearest neighbors who are of the other faction and live next door.

These days, the people of Northern Ireland enjoy an absence of conflict and violence, and the walls are in part responsible for this. But true peace, justice for all, the welfare of Belfast, and the flourishing that human community is meant to entail are no closer than when the peace walls were first built.

Peace depends on understanding. Justice requires empathy. Flourishing demands commitment to the deep relationships that make understanding and empathy possible. Whether in Belfast or Baltimore, what is needed are bridges of trust, not walls of distrust.

Trust has to be earned, and that can be done in many ways. One of the ways I think best is through advocacy: speaking with marginalized people as they seek justice. Justice sought alongside someone on the margins because of race, economics, gender, or nationality is a powerful tool when done in partnership with them. Advocating with friends is a transformative process for everyone involved.

Jesus himself tore down walls and built bridges—in Samaria, in Canaan, and at Matthew's house, for example—as he exemplified what it means to live a life of justice for all, not just for those people we assumed he would be more easily inclined to love. We cannot get to justice without the messiness of advocating for those who are different from us. Jesus brings us together by getting rid of walls, but justice usually only happens where we establish common need and are willing to walk through issues of injustice together.

I've spent quite a bit of time going to places and listening to people from all backgrounds as they struggle for justice, whether it's in the midst of women making decisions to be free from sex-trafficking in Bolivia or young people protesting in Ferguson, Missouri, for freedom. As we listen, advocate, and lend our voices, we can begin to see hope in the eyes of those standing with their backs against walls, and we are drawn to stand alongside them. If we get close enough, we'll see people just like us longing to live in ways in which their humanity is not denied. But first we must get close enough. When relationships lack depth, justice remains only a distant wish. Walls don't work, because inevitably we need each other and we need to hear and understand each other's stories. In many cases, if we were closer to people across cultures the workload would be lighter.

Peace with one another will move us towards justice. When we respect each other as human beings and move into relationships across cultures and with the hard folks in our lives, systems of injustice can be transformed. This is where relationships can play a huge role in justice. For example, it will be possible to create equal education for all children when we know and have relationships with families who, because they are in poor communities, are underserved by our education systems. We won't just want to help "the poor," but we will care about those among the poor we have taken the time to get to know. The people we know get the benefit of doubt based on the relationships we share with them.

JUSTICE REQUIRES NAMING INJUSTICE

It's not enough, though, to just bridge the gaps and get connected with people who need advocates for justice. The reality is that it's just not possible to see justice take shape without confrontation. If you are the recipient of injustice, part of your freedom comes in being enabled to bring your story to light. In the naming of injustice people are held accountable to treat everyone equally or are called out for not doing so. This is a hard reality for many and, quite frankly, it's the reason why peace seems to be eluding us in so many places. Racism continues to rage, crises around the world are increasing, and our efforts to solve problems through military might and political negotiations fall far short.

Injustice clearly suggests that an inequality of some type exists. Injustice is an identifier and admission that a wrong has been committed. It acknowledges that there has been bias, and that that bias gave someone an unfair advantage and disadvantaged someone else. We all have biases, and we are not very good at treating everyone equally, so we all need accountability. We see injustice in many ways around the world—in hiring practices, housing, access to food, water, or education based on race, gender, nationality, or religion. Justice means simply correcting the things that are wrong.

We are absolutely called to confront injustice. Sometimes it seems like we want to have justice without taking the risk of calling out what's wrong. Calling out an injustice is one of the strongest ways to show advocacy and care for the marginalized. Sometimes people just need the record set straight. I remember many days in ministry when I was being openly mistreated as the only black person in a meeting or at an event. I can state with confidence that those who suffer from injustice want the wrong called out and corrected. But no one confronted my oppressor. And when confrontation is lacking, it leads to all kinds of mistrust. It can seem like there is a protection of the oppressor at the expense of the oppressed.

I remember when we gathered a few teams to help with disaster relief after hurricane Katrina. There were several people who came to serve for an entire year, many of whom were female and people of color. Roscoe was an older gentleman who also volunteered to be there and was put in charge of our teams. Roscoe didn't have much experience with diversity and had a very bad demeanor toward some of the women. He used all kinds of racial slurs and made degrading statements toward women, especially women of color. I asked that someone confront Roscoe after an incident where he put a young Latina woman in a dangerous position and used a racial slur toward her and the people she was working with. Although many agreed he should be removed from leadership and asked to leave, it was done ever so carefully and quietly. Do I believe people wanted to protect Roscoe at the expense of the persons affected? No. But were they further hurt and humiliated at the amount of care shown to his atrocious behavior? Yes they were. I don't think he should have been publicly whipped or shamed, but he should have been confronted quickly and dismissed right away for insulting and demeaning someone. When we don't speak out and act quickly, we raise questions of solidarity with the oppressor.

My friend Jeremy Courtney lives in this tension. He works in Iraq with the organization Preemptive Love, a global movement of peacemakers that is changing the way we engage the world's most polarizing conflicts by confronting fear with acts of love. At the core of each conflict is fear. We fear ideas and religions. We fear loss, shame, and the unknown. So we fight. First, with attitudes and words, and then with fists and guns. Violence, mistrust, and rivalry result in injustice for our children and our future. But Jeremy and Preemptive Love are working to change this dynamic.

For Jeremy, it all began during the Iraq War in the Iraqi city where he'd moved with his wife and daughter. While Jeremy was working at his computer in a hotel lobby, an Iraqi father approached him wondering, *What if this foreigner could help my sick daughter?* Jeremy, in turn, wondered, *What if I could?*

"What if" is a beautiful phrase. It is the heartbeat of innovation and risk, where rebellion and hope meet, and it has the power to remake the world. That first "What if" set the Preemptive Love team on the path toward reconciliation, providing lifesaving surgeries and essential aid for the sake of bringing greater equality to communities and waging peace.

Although the people of Iraq are now Jeremy's friends, they didn't start out that way. Justice was pursued beyond borders and the norm. Justice was seen as a must even in tough places. Pursuing what is right outside of our comfort zones may not be as easy as we want but it's in line with representing the God we love and know. We can choose to be brave and go beyond our safe zones to be part of the work of justice. We can be like that Iraqi father in a hotel lobby all those years ago who believed things could change, but we have to be willing to do the work of making justice come alive.

8

LOVING EVEN OUR ENEMIES

But I tell you, love your enemies and pray for those who persecute you, that you may be children of your Father in heaven.

Matthew 5:44-45

On a Wednesday evening on the seventeenth of June at Emanuel AME in Charleston, South Carolina, nine people were killed while they studied the Bible and prayed in their church. The person responsible was a young man, only twenty-one years old, named Dylann Roof. He was there at the Bible study for almost an hour before he opened fire and then drove away. Eight people died in the church that evening and another person died later.

The reports went out describing the assailant as a white male who was armed and dangerous. One surviving witness gave testimony that the assailant left her alive to tell the story.

Roof was quoted as saying, "You all rape women and you're taking over our country." He then added, "I have to do what I have to do." At the end of the Bible study, Roof began shooting as people were praying. This was a ruthless racially motivated killing in a church. There is no question that this was calculated, hateful, racist, and evil.

FORGIVENESS

Roof was captured and stood in court on a Friday morning to hear the charges being brought against him for the deaths of nine people. But the families of the victims had a message they wanted to send to Roof and the world: it was a lesson in forgiveness. I listened to the family members of those murdered and I was stunned. "You took something very precious away from me. . . . I will never talk to her ever again. I will never be able to hold her again. But I forgive you and have mercy on your soul. You hurt me. You hurt a lot of people, but I forgive you." Felicia Sanders, who survived the shooting by pretending to be dead, also spoke about losing her son in the attack: "Tywanza was my hero. . . . May God have mercy on you." Bethane Middleton-Brown, whose sister had been killed, told Roof, "For me, I'm a work in progress and I acknowledge that I'm very angry. We have no room for hate. We have to forgive. I pray God on your soul." Chris Singleton, son of one of the victims, said, "We've come together as a community to try to get past these things. A tragedy has happened, but life is going to go on and things are going to get better."

God commanded Israel to pray for Babylon. This connects directly to the message of Jesus when he commands us to pray for those who persecute (or despitefully use) us. Israel was indeed being persecuted, and yet God called them to a spirit of prayer—to pray for Babylon's success.

It is of utmost importance that we see our call to crosscultural relationships as spiritual engagement. The power and ability to love hard people and places does not come from our human will. Our human will is selfish and without depth. It's when we engage the power of Christ that we can love others in ways that encourage them and us together.

As I mentioned in chapter three, the Trinity is a beautiful example of relationship that calls us into relational space with God that goes deeper than we can imagine on our own. We were created by a relational God, one who is a community of three persons. The *imago Dei* is communal. We also, therefore, were made for and long for relationship. We were not meant to be alone. But our fallen world—particularly the American version—pushes us to live as individuals, which runs counter to the way we were made. At our very core, we need each other. Loneliness is a prescription for death, but when we are in community, we thrive. There is power to be found in community. It's a power that goes further than anything we can accomplish alone. Togetherness is so much a part of God's plan for us that he even tells us to love our enemies.

Look, I know this sounds absolutely crazy and it isn't always the most practical idea. When we're angry and can't rush into forgiveness, I get it. I've had the hardest time forgiving my dad for many things and the hardest time forgiving stupid comments made by white folks from the time I was very young, but I cannot be completely alone. There are major cultural issues, power dynamics, and a nasty history to work through, but I believe that we are our best selves together. We know and represent humanity and our Creator best as one. By "one" I don't mean monocultural. I mean a dynamic expression of different people connected and embracing—embracing to solve problems, to represent all people, and to celebrate differences. This may sound like a dream scenario given where we are today, but it's a goal worth fighting for. The families that forgave in Charleston were a reminder of how radical forgiveness can be. The words of Jesus:

> But to you who are listening I say: Love your enemies, do good to those who hate you, bless those who curse you, pray for those who mistreat you. If someone slaps you on one cheek, turn to them the other also. If someone takes your coat, do not withhold your shirt from them. Give to everyone who asks you, and if anyone takes what belongs to you, do not demand it back. Do to others as you would have them do to you. (Lk 6:27-31)

This teaching suggests that we are to try to establish relationships with the other, even with those who hate us. It's natural for us to focus on our own welfare and the welfare of our families—we put away treasure for ourselves and seek after our own futures. There is nothing wrong with these things per se, but the single-mindedness in which we pursue our own, protect our own, and love our own must be examined in light of the brokenness in the world around us. God's call is much more radical: that all people and relationships matter, even our enemies.

A DIFFICULT COMMAND

Of all the Bible's commands, those verses in Luke are probably some of the most difficult for Christians to keep. How many times have you heard of someone dealing with the person that stole from them by giving the thief more? Where have you heard of someone not demanding what was taken? Jesus' idea is not just about offering forgiveness or overlooking the offense, but also investing in the person that hurt you.

We follow these verses least when it comes to strangers in our lives and we follow them deeply when there is family or a relationship involved. The friend or child who steals money from you is much more likely to be forgiven than the stranger at a mall who takes your pocketbook. And yet, Jesus' expectations don't include allowance for such a double standard:

> If you love those who love you, what credit is that to you? Even sinners love those who love them. And if you do good to those who are good to you, what credit is that to you? Even sinners do that. And if you lend to those from whom you expect repayment, what credit is that to you? Even sinners lend to sinners, expecting to be repaid in full. But love your enemies, do good to them, and lend to them without expecting to get anything back. Then your reward will be great, and you will be children of the Most High, because he is kind to the ungrateful and wicked. Be merciful, just as your Father is merciful. (Lk 6:32-36)

God sent Israel into exile and then told them to pray for Babylon. The Babylonians were the very people who had just killed their families, taken their homes, and forced them to walk for hundreds of miles to a remote land. This word from the Lord was not easy at all. In fact, it's absolutely crazy in the world's economy. It's much easier to hate whatever category of people you feel has wronged you or you fear: a particular race of people, men, your dad, gays, immigrants, and the person or group whose sin against you has marked your life.

The idea that being a follower of Jesus requires walking in love and forgiveness as a way of life is incomprehensible for many. But it seems to be a non-negotiable principle of both Jesus' life and teaching. The fact that it remains inconceivable for so many Christians is a big part of why we still see so much division in our world today. We have not really tapped into this part of God's plan for reconciliation. We have not truly accepted the radical kingdom's ways. The power of the Trinity remains elusive for many of us because we don't see this radical love as plausible in our lives—we don't believe God had our particular enemies and our unique hurts in mind when he spoke those words.

We want justice and change but we must be willing to model it as well. We have to be willing to live a radically spiritual life, and the most radical thing we can do is give to an enemy. This changes us and our enemies and moves the seemingly immovable needle. Dr. King said that love drives out hate. Profound love is an act that is unmatched in the world.

IF SOMEONE TAKES YOUR COAT . . .

Marquis was a kid in our youth group. He was a challenge, for sure, but we had come to know him and to appreciate him as a child of God. While Donna and I were away, Marquis was pressured by a few other boys in the neighborhood to join them as they kicked down our front door and began robbing our house. Marquis, who started feeling guilty, stood by and watched as it happened. Our neighbors next door saw what was going on, called the police, and described the boys involved.

My wife and I came home to a trashed house and to reports from neighbors that Marquis was involved and in jail. I went to Marquis's house to see his mom, who was extremely apologetic. She also told us that Donna and I were the only ones who were making a positive influence in her son's life, and she asked if I could take her to the jail and help bail him out. In my mind, I thought, *Really? You want me to go help bail out the guy who robbed my house? Really?* But God answered yes. An hour later, I found myself at the jail, talking to a repentant Marquis (who hadn't himself stolen anything but was highly involved).

The next week, Marquis was before the juvenile court and I was subpoenaed as the victim. The prosecutor asked me whether I felt safe going into court since we lived a block from the perpetrator. I told him I felt safe, and then began to tell him that I was a local pastor and neighborhood leader. I requested that Marquis be assigned to me for community service in lieu of jail time. The prosecutor looked at me as if I was from Mars, but then said I would need to ask the judge.

The judge asked Marquis and me to stand. He then asked the prosecutor what sentence he was asking the court to hand down. When the prosecutor explained that the victim, Mr. Barber, wished that the perpetrator, Marquis, be assigned to him for community service, the judge looked confused. He held up the list of all the stuff we had lost from our home, as if I needed a reminder. He asked whether I believed and understood that Marquis was involved in the crime, and I acknowledged that I did. He asked Marquis if he was present at the robbery, and he confessed that he was. The judge asked again whether I was requesting that Marquis be turned over to me. When I confirmed that that was my desire, he shook his head and turned to Marquis. "Son," he said, "I don't know why, but I will sentence you to thirty days of community service with Reverend Barber."

Marquis and his mom were elated, and I couldn't believe the judge actually did it. Standing up for your enemy changes the rules in the room. It makes people rethink situations and give an opportunity for love to rule the moment. Love definitely ruled this moment. We were all challenged to live differently and to see grace as an option on the table where it usually isn't. My relationship with this family deepened and it caused other relationships around the neighborhood to deepen. I began getting requests from parents to talk to sons and to step in when moms felt overwhelmed. I can't say all those relationships have led to a great ending, but what I can say is they have shown a neighborhood, families, and a court system that there are other possibilities for restoration.

A CAVEAT

Obviously, loving our enemies will not always cause them to repay us with love or automatically bring about their redemption and transformation. Some will be unresponsive, unwilling to repent, and much less, change. I'm not so naive as to believe that there's a simple equation between our treatment of our enemies and their response to that treatment.

Jesus' teachings include a balancing principle that acknowledges this. There may come a time when our best efforts at loving the difficult person is the equivalent of "casting pearls before swine." So our Lord's words to his original twelve disciples as he sent them out into ministry have application for us today:

> As you enter the home, give it your greeting. If the home is deserving, let your peace rest on it; if it is not, let your peace return to you. If anyone will not welcome you or listen to your words, leave that home or town and shake the dust off your feet. (Mt 10:12-14)

But that point comes only after we have initiated relationship and tried. It doesn't come by sitting at home or across a wall and projecting what the other's response will be. We first have to go and give relationship a chance. We have to provide opportunity for Christ-like, Spirit-powered understanding, forgiveness, love, and reconciliation to do supernatural work.

Let's be honest. Have we done a good job of entering into awkward relationships? Have we placed the emphasis on Christ's command to go seeking reconciliation, or have we exercised the "out" of expecting a hard-hearted response? Have we been doing all that we can to allow the love and grace of Christ to flow through us to reach the hard people with whom he has placed us? Have we been faithful ambassadors of our Lord's kingdom in the hard places, or have we tended to ignore the mission he's given us?

Are our challenging neighborhoods and hard cities better because of the Christian presence in them—because of *our* presence in them?

STILL TOO MUCH TO ASK

I understand the objection that comes at this point, and it's a legitimate one. I have experienced some horrible traumas myself, but maybe not the ones that you have. As a pastor, I've heard personal stories of unimaginable, life-scarring, soul-wrenching grievances. Some of my readers have been raped, or experienced physical, sexual, or psychological abuse at the hands of the people that brought them into the world.

The obvious question is, *God can't really expect me to forgive* that, *can he?*

I admit that I don't know the pain of your personal situation. And I can't conceive of how difficult it would be to forgive those responsible for what you've been through. But as a pastor and a person who has had to forgive, with all my heart I believe that Christ knows what he's talking about when he asks us to forgive as we've been forgiven. "Forgive us our sins, for we also forgive everyone who sins against us" (Lk 11:4).

I can offer you examples of Christians who, despite being the victims of horrible acts, have allowed God's forgiveness to flow through them to the perpetrators of those crimes. I've mentioned the family members of those recently murdered in Charleston: each of those who expressed forgiveness to Dylann Roof took Christ at his word and, under some of the most difficult circumstances imaginable, chose not to let bitterness and anger rule their lives, but to extend forgiveness and to seek reconciliation and relationship.

Now let me mention Célestin Musekura and the pastors and people of African Leadership and Reconciliation Ministries (ALARM). Most of us are aware of the horrific genocide that occurred in the 1990s in Rwanda, in which Hutus and Tutsis warred against one another in an escalating ethnic conflict. Célestin, a pastor and community leader, was living in Kenya for seminary training when his home village was destroyed by this violence. He returned home to find his family missing. He later found them alive in one of many refugee camps. It was in the refugee camp that he felt God call him to a ministry of leadership formation and to a life of seeking peace and reconciliation among the warring factions. He based this ministry on the life and teachings of Jesus about forgiving others, including our enemies.

For several years—during which Célestin was himself beaten three times by people from his own tribe and tortured on one occasion by government authorities—Christ's message of peace and reconciliation was shared among pastors, community leaders, and ordinary people affected by the fighting. Then in 1997, five members of his family and seventy members of the church he pastored were slain in revenge for earlier killings. Now Christ's command to forgive came home to Célestin in a new and deeply personal way. As he obeyed that command, eventually forgiving and embracing the very men responsible for the deaths of his family and flock, Célestin experienced the supernatural blessing and freedom of forgiveness and peace in Christ.

SELFLESS LOVE

Christ not only commands us as his followers to forgive our enemies—he showed us the way. Jesus understands what it means to be abused and rejected. The physical, emotional, and spiritual pain he experienced on that Roman cross (and during the events leading up to it) was as unjust and horrific as anything imaginable. Jesus understands your pain and the unfairness of it. And yet, he chose to forgive his enemies, even in the middle of an excruciating ordeal: "Father, forgive them, for they do not know what they are doing" (Lk 23:34).

But here's the reality, and the really important thing: Jesus not only exemplifies selfless love and forgiveness of enemies, but makes it possible in our lives. As fallen people, the best love we can achieve falls short of the mark. We cannot of our own accord extend forgiveness to others in circumstances like those we've discussed. It's only God's Spirit indwelling us that makes such radical love and forgiveness possible. But for those of us who recognize Christ's sacrifice on our behalf and the forgiveness and grace the Father has extended to us, refusing to do the same for others is not the response God is looking for.

We need to get busy with the task of reconciliation with all those around us, including those who have hurt us the most. Our troubled world needs us to be Christ's ambassadors of reconciliation. One area in which the church can pursue this call is to better understand a burgeoning movement that is widely misunderstood: Black Lives Matter. We'll take time to better understand this movement in the next chapter.

Love is an action and not always a gushy feeling. So how can you take action to love your enemy? Buy your enemy lunch, even if it's challenging. Send an anonymous gift or flowers. Compliment something your enemy does well. These are small actions that, if done over time, may be able to change our hearts. Wanting our enemy to fail is quite natural, but we must do things that push us toward grace. What pushes us toward grace best is when we understand another's story with ourselves in mind. We must imagine how we would want to be treated in such situations and then treat our enemy the same way—this is what it means to embrace even those that we might say we hate. This is the heart of the gospel.

9

YES, BLACK LIVES MATTER!

You are worthy to take the scroll
and to open its seals,
because you were slain,
and with your blood you purchased for God
persons from every tribe and language and people and nation.
You have made them to be a kingdom
and priests to serve our God,
and they will reign on the earth.

REVELATION 5:9-10

My heart dropped as I watched the face of Michael Brown's mother and listened to her screams as she looked upon her son lying in the street, not being allowed to approach his body. His dead body lay there for four hours and his mom, family, and friends looked on with horror. The scene was played over and over and the more it played, the more it seemed as though the life of this young man meant nothing. Many had that same thought and #BlackLivesMatter captured it. The scene of

Michael Brown's death, along with many others, was the catalyst to the creation of #BlackLivesMatter. The statement was needed to remind us that we did indeed matter, even if only to ourselves. We are declaring it for ourselves, for our children, and for generations to come.

The Black Lives Matter movement is currently causing controversy and debate, even within the church. InterVarsity Christian Fellowship weathered quite a bit of criticism when #BlackLivesMatter was highlighted at the Urbana 15 Student Missions Conference. Some Christians wonder how we can embrace a movement that seems in certain ways to uphold values that are contrary to Christian ideals. Why should the church, some ask, care about BLM when its agenda seems to be suspicious and even dangerous? But perhaps we need to look at the emergence of BLM in another way: as a part of God's plan to bring us into relationship with one another across race and cultural barriers.

Revelation 5 pictures all of God's people together worshiping the Lamb who was slain on our behalf. On that day we will together make up a kingdom of priests, and that kingdom will be composed of people from every language, ethnicity, culture, and nationality. The barriers that divide us will be gone, though the skin colors and speech that distinguish us will remain. Indeed, the very diversity that now causes us so much trouble will then be a notable part of the glory and wonder of our combined worship.

To be sure, the picture in Revelation 5 is of a future time. But that future reality is far truer than our present tumultuous attempts to just get along. The reality is that our lives are bound together in God's kingdom and that we can together begin to experience his ultimate plans even now.

The text says that they will reign on the earth. The location of this glorious future reality is right here, where we're living now. Can we imagine for a moment what this will look like—our barrios and neighborhoods being places of uninterrupted shalom, our slums and "projects" lush and beautiful centers of human flourishing, our war-torn cities and countrysides gardens of peace and joy?

It seems pretty clear that we have not yet experienced all that God has for us as a redeemed and reconciled community of believers. It is time we started reaching across the barriers that continue to separate us.

DEBUNKING THE MYTHS OF #BLACKLIVESMATTER

The Black Lives Matter movement was born out of the continued struggle of black people in the United States and around the world. It's a call for blacks to be respected as human beings. This movement has given voice to many who are being oppressed and denied rights that should be given to all people. I have felt this violation of basic human rights profoundly as I've watched men and women killed in the streets by police—with many of these participating officers not even having to answer in court. Black Lives Matter seems to have sparked a resurgence of the civil rights movement and features a younger generation who is taking ownership. Although the movement understands the history of civil rights and the role of the church, it has decided to do some things differently. This has come under major scrutiny from many. There has been a great deal of misunderstanding about #BLM, and I would like to debunk some of the myths and misunderstandings that surround it.

Myth number 1: The movement doesn't care about black-on-black crime. The idea that black-on-black crime is not a significant political conversation among black people is patently false. In Chicago, long maligned for its high rates of intraracial murder, members of the community have created the Violence Interrupters to disrupt violent altercations before they escalate. Those who still insist on talking about black-on-black crime frequently fail to acknowledge that most crime is intraracial. 93 percent of black murder victims are killed by other black people. 84 percent of white murder victims are killed by other white people. The continued focus on black-on-black crime is a diversionary tactic whose goal is to suggest that black people don't have the right to be outraged about police violence in vulnerable black communities just because those communities have a crime problem. The Black Lives Matter movement acknowledges the crime problem, but it refuses to locate that crime problem as a problem of black pathology. Black people are not inherently more violent or more prone to crime than other groups. But black people are disproportionately poorer, more likely to be targeted by police and arrested, and more likely to attend poor or failing schools. All of these social indicators place a black person at greater risk for being either a victim or a perpetrator of violent crime. To reduce violent crime, we must fight to change systems rather than demonizing people.

Myth number 2: It's a leaderless movement. The Black Lives Matter movement is a *leaderfull* movement. Many Americans of all races are enamored with Martin Luther King Jr. as a symbol of leadership and of what real movements look like. But the Movement for Black Lives (another name for the BLM movement) recognizes many flaws with this model. First, focusing on heterosexual, cisgender black men frequently causes us not to see the significant amount of labor and thought leadership that black women provide to movements, not only in caretaking and auxiliary roles, but on the front lines of protests and in the strategy sessions that happen behind closed doors. Moreover, those old models of leadership favored the old over the young, attempted to silence gay and lesbian leadership, and did not recognize the leadership possibilities of transgender people at all. A movement with a singular leader or few visible leaders is vulnerable, because those leaders can be easily identified, harassed, and killed, as was the case with Dr. King. But by having a *leaderfull* movement, BLM addresses many of these concerns. BLM is composed of many local leaders and many local organizations including Black Youth Project 100, the Dream Defenders, the Organization for Black Struggle, Hands Up United, Millennial Activists United, and the Black Lives Matter national network. We demonstrate through this model that the movement is bigger than any one person. And there is room for the talents, expertise, and work ethic of anyone who is committed to freedom.

Myth number 3: The movement has no agenda. Many believe the Black Lives Matter movement has no agenda—other than yelling and protesting and disrupting the lives of white people. This is also false. Since the earliest days of the movement in Ferguson, groups like the Organization for Black Struggle, the Black Lives Matter network, and others have made a clear and public list of demands. Those demands include swift and transparent legal investigation of all police shootings of black people, official governmental tracking of the number of citizens killed by police (disaggregated by race), the demilitarization of local police forces, and community accountability mechanisms for rogue police officers. Some proposals like the recently launched Campaign Zero by a group of Ferguson activists call for body cameras on every police officer. But other groups are more reticent about this solution, since it would lead to increased surveillance and possible invasions of privacy, not to mention a massive governmental database of information about communities of color that are already heavily under surveillance by government forces.

Myth number 4: It's a one-issue movement. Although it is true that much of the protesting to date has been centered on the issue of police brutality, there's a range of issues that the movement will likely push in years to come. One is the issue of our failing public education system, which is a virtual school-to-prison pipeline for many black youth. Another is the complete dismantling of the prison industrial complex. Many of the movement's organizers identify as abolitionists, which in the twenty-first-century context refers to people who want to abolish prisons and end the problem of mass incarceration of black and Latino people. Three other significant issues are problems with safe and affordable housing, issues with food security, and reproductive-justice challenges affecting poor women of color and all people needing access to reproductive care. As I frequently like to tell people, this movement in its current iteration is still very new. Things take time to mold and take shape. Give it some time to find its footing and its take on all the aforementioned issues. But the conversations are on the table largely because many of the folks doing work on the ground came to this movement through their organizing work around other issues.

Myth number 5: The movement has no respect for elders. The BLM movement is an intergenerational movement. If you ever have occasion to attend a protest action, you will see black people of all ages, from the very young to the very old, standing in solidarity with the work being done. Certainly there have been schisms and battles between younger and older movers about tactics and strategies. There has also been criticism from prior civil rights participants. BLM has a clear rejection of the respectability politics ethos of the civil rights era, namely a belief in the idea that proper dress and speech will guard blacks against harassment by the police. This is a significant point of tension within black communities, because in a system that makes one feel powerless to change it, belief in the idea that a good job, being well-behaved, and having proper dress and comportment will protect you from the evils of racism makes it feel like there's something you can do to protect yourself, that there's something you can do to have a bit of control over your destiny. This movement patently rejects such thinking in the face of the massive evidence of police mistreatment of black people across all classes and backgrounds. All people should be treated with dignity and respect, regardless of how one looks or speaks.

Myth number 6: The black church has no role to play. Many know that the black church was central to the civil rights movement, since many black male preachers became prominent civil rights leaders. This current movement has a very different relationship to the church than in movements past. Black churches and black preachers in Ferguson have been on the ground helping since the early days after Michael Brown's death. But protesters patently reject any conservative theology that focuses on keeping the peace, praying copiously, or turning the other cheek. Such calls are viewed as a return to passive respectability politics. But local preachers and pastors like Rev. Traci Blackmon, Rev. Starsky Wilson, and Rev. Osagyefo Sekou have emerged as what I call "Movement Pastors." With their radical theologies of inclusion and investment in preaching a revolutionary Jesus (a focus on the parts of Scripture where Jesus challenges the Roman power structure) and their willingness to think of church beyond the bounds of a physical structure or traditional worship, they are reimagining what notions of faith and church look like and radically transforming the idea of what the twenty-first-century black church should be.

Myth number 7: The movement hates white people. The statement "black lives matter" is not an anti-white proposition. Contained within the statement is an unspoken but implied "too," as in "black lives matter, too," which suggests that the statement is one of inclusion rather than exclusion. However, those white people who continue to mischaracterize the affirmation as being anti-white are suggesting that in order for white lives to matter, black lives cannot. That is a foundational premise of white supremacy. It is antithetical to what the Black Lives Matter movement stands for, which is the simple proposition that black lives *also* matter. The Black Lives Matter movement demands that the country affirm the value of black life in practical and pragmatic ways, including addressing an increasing racial wealth gap, fixing public schools that are failing, combating issues of housing inequality and gentrification that continue to push people of color out of communities where they have lived in for generations, and dismantling the prison industrial complex. None of this is about hatred for white life. It is about acknowledging that the system already treats white lives as if they have more value, as if they are more worthy of protection, safety, education, and a good quality of life than black lives are. This must change.

Myth number 8: The movement hates police officers. Police officers are people. Their lives have inherent value. This movement is not an anti-people movement; therefore, it is not an anti-police-officer movement. Most police officers are just everyday people who want to do their jobs, make a living for their families, and come home safely at the end of their shift. This does not mean, however, that police are not implicated in a system that criminalizes black people, that demands that they view black people as unsafe and dangerous, that trains them to be more aggressive and less accommodating with black citizens, and that does not stress that we are taxpayers who deserve to be protected and served just like everyone else. Thus the Black Lives Matter movement is not trying to make the world more unsafe for police officers; it hopes to make police officers less of a threat to communities of color. We reject the idea that asking officers questions about why one is being stopped or arrested, about what one is being charged with, constitutes either disrespect or resistance. We reject the use of military-grade weapons as appropriate policing mechanisms for any American community. We reject the faulty idea that disrespect is a crime, that black people should be nice or civil when they are being hassled or arrested on trumped-up charges. And we question the idea that police officers should be given the benefit of the doubt when it comes to policing black communities. Increasingly, the presence of police makes black people feel less rather than more safe. And that has everything to do with the antagonistic and power-laden ways in which police interact with citizens generally and black citizens in particular. Police officers must rebuild trust with the communities they police. Not the other way around.

Myth number 9: The movement's primary goal should be the vote. Recently the Democratic National Committee endorsed the Black Lives Matter movement. The BLM network swiftly rejected that endorsement. While voting certainly matters, particularly in local municipalities like Ferguson, movement members are clear that voting for policies and politicians whose ultimate goal is to maintain a rotten and unjust system is counterproductive. The movement cares about national politics, and many participants have sought to make presidential candidates responsive to their political concerns. But there is deep skepticism about whether the American system is salvageable, since it's so deeply rooted in ideas of racial caste. In this regard, the BLM movement, together with the Occupy movement of years past, is causing a resurgence of a viable, visible, and vocal (black) left in national politics. Moving some issues of import onto the 2016 election agenda should therefore be viewed as a tactic, not a goal. The goal is freedom and safety for all black lives. And that goal is much bigger than one election.

Myth number 10: There's not actually a movement at all. Until Bernie Sanders sought the attention of Black Lives Matter participants, many were unwilling to acknowledge that a new racial justice movement even existed. For the record, since August 2014, there have been more than 1,030 protest actions held in the name of Black Lives Matter. We should take notice of this new generation of freedom fighters as they make their mark in history. A new generation of protest music has come forth, with songs from Janelle Monae, Prince, J. Cole, Lauryn Hill, and Rick Ross. The first national convening in July drew over one thousand participants. There is a new consciousness and a new spirit seeking justice, and the participants carrying the torch show no signs of slowing down.

I'm aware that there are challenges for some Christians when it comes to Black Lives Matter. I am not saying (and neither do I believe they are saying) that you have to agree with everything. Giving support to BLM doesn't mean you agree with everything—there are differing opinions even within the movement itself. What we should agree on is that this movement has helped bring voice to the frustrations and feelings of many black people who have felt neglected, looked past, and ignored as human beings. The need to feel seen as a person is real.

I am not requesting that you agree with everything you have read about Black Lives Matter. I am advocating for a listening ear, healthy dialogue, and love. This is where loving hard people—including our enemies—begins to take shape in our hearts. Can you love and disagree? Can you love and honor another's humanity in spite of the differences?

FOR THOSE WHO ARE NOT BLACK

I recently talked to a white, male, middle-aged friend and leader in the nonprofit world, and he confessed that there is no one black in his inner circles, and for that matter, not a single person of color. This was a lament, and in it he was truly confessing and wanting to repent. He wanted to start again.

The big question then was how. How does a white man in his fifties make new friends? It's hard for anyone to look outside their social circles for new friends, and it's is especially hard for middle-aged folks like him and me.

This is one of the more insidious things about racism in America. We don't fully know how to engage outside our own circles. This has caused injustice to burn out of control and racism to run rampant, paralyzing us when it comes to practical ways to find reconciliation.

But there are ways to start. Here's a list of suggestions:

- Read books written by blacks and discuss them.
- Shop in a mall or store on the other side of town routinely.

- Watch different TV shows.
- Listen to a different radio station.
- Go to a different coffee shop.
- Go see movies with mostly black casts.
- Attend a black church routinely (once a month or quarter).
- Give to an organization led by a person of color.
- Go see a play written and performed by black writers and actors.
- Visit the African American museum close to you.
- Go to a sporting event with a black coworker at your place of employment.
- Take your church small group to a protest or rally.
- Set up regular prayer time or attend a prayer meeting at a black church.
- Put your kids in an activity where they will interact with black children.

Please don't get me wrong. We have some very deep racial problems and injustice to work through, and these things are by no means the answer. But they may at least move us a step closer in understanding by creating space for new friendships to emerge.

TAKING THE TIME

I've thought about why certain people seem to be able to embrace those who are different, whereas others struggle with getting along. It seems to me that the most important factor is patience—that the people who succeed at getting past differences and misunderstandings are those willing to take the time to get to know other people.

Those who embrace others don't let stereotypes or even their own experiences predetermine the possibilities for new relationships. They risk getting to know someone even when it might be dangerous. They disregard the misplaced counsel of their close friends who think the idea of engaging others who are different is impossible or foolish. They ignore the racist taunts and name-calling that might come along with taking risks for relationships and for having the ideal that perhaps we can get to a new place. They accept that the world may misunderstand them. They remain anchored to the certain knowledge that God will bless their obedience and will reveal a bit more of himself in the other person they are called to love.

Embracing the call to relationships means . . .

- taking time to get to know one another.
- taking time to trust one another.
- taking time to see things in a new way.
- seeking to enjoy another person's ways when they differ from our own.
- wanting what is right even if that means being alone and misunderstood.
- being true and honest about who our friends are even when they are from the other side of the tracks.
- loving deeply even when we don't always understand.
- praying for the person who hurts us.
- giving to something we don't fully understand because friendship is more important.

- going against our own culture for the sake of a friend.
- celebrating with strangers.
- being vulnerable in a strange place.
- listening to one another's stories even when don't understand.
- even being willing to die for those you consider your enemy.

All of these things enable us to start loving people we once hated. They allow us to start going to places we would never have gone before. We risk going into unfamiliar places in pursuit of true community. But once we achieve true community, we find we have new places where we are known, loved, and appreciated, where we accept advice from unlikely sources and where improbable people take risks for our sakes.

It's all good, it's all sweet, it's all risky, and it's all somehow possible.

The promise of Revelation 5 only eludes us because we aren't willing to go the distance with people who are different from us. I believe with all my heart that our joy in loving community is incomplete if that community is monocultural. We can only know God's full blessing when we are loving *all* of our neighbors, when we have put Christ's kingdom first, ahead of our prejudices, our comfort, and our culture's ways. We can and must love the Samaritans, the Babylonians, and the Ninevites in our lives.

What a testimony that would be for the world around us! The mark of the follower of Christ is love for one another. But the world is not impressed by those who love only their own family, their own tribe or fraternity. It's when we allow the love of Christ in us to be expressed through us to those of other ethnicities and nationalities that the unbelieving culture will sit up and take notice.

This is why the case of love and forgiveness by the Charleston families moves us so much. When we see the forgiveness of Jacob DeShazer toward his Japanese captors, we recognize the supernatural in it. We know that the compassion of African American slave women for the children of their masters is not a purely human thing, but that Christ's love animates it. When we understand that the relatives of Jim Elliot and Nate Saint gave the rest of their lives to bring God's love to the tribal people who killed them, we stand in awe in the presence of the Prince of Peace.

I've had glimpses in my own life of the supernatural joy of loving those who are vastly different from me. I've seen many who have taken chances and come out on the other side with incredible relationships that last a lifetime. My life has been made so much fuller by loving different people from around the world and across the street.

Why don't you give it a shot? Why don't you grab an opportunity to go to a place where you're not supposed to be? Why don't you invest your time and treasures in a relationship? Why don't you become foolish in the world's eyes to see if the impossible can come to life? We are all one people, and we have more in common than we think. We just don't push ourselves to embrace those commonalities. Our culture and forces all around us tell us not to trust, not to reach across those walls, not to listen to one another's stories, not to consider the other side of the story, not to believe God's picture of his kingdom on earth. What if God meant for us to find our true selves only in relationship with one another? What if all we have to do is take a step toward those relationships—and then God will manifest the power that raised Christ from the dead?

I know the road before us is not going to be easy. I expect it to be filled with hard places and difficult people. The work involved may seem overwhelming as we press for unity, peace, and equality. But we know what the end could look like—what God has shown us in Revelation 5. This doesn't mean moving past the hard relationships too quickly, or discounting the need for the difficult confrontation of systems of power and injustice. In fact, we need to enter into this with eyes wide open, fully aware of the trials inherent to such a commitment to relationship.

We are in the middle of a very divisive moment. The winds of discord are blowing hard. We are in a conflict-ridden conversation and it's troublesome. But our current way of living and relating will only lead to destruction. There is hope, and that hope rests in our ability to honor one another in the strength of deep relationship. We'll use one of the most powerful Forces we know to weave us into harmony, and allow the essence of our cultures, creativity, and hearts to help us solve our largest problems. We are God's creation, made from one place. We are different because God is so vast, alike because he is one. Let's embrace the Spirit of God that rests in us all.

ACKNOWLEDGMENTS

This book would not have been possible without the help and guidance of so many people. I will never be able to thank you enough.

To Donna, my amazing wife: Thank you for being such a supportive partner, appreciating and understanding my entrepreneurial ways. You are so beautiful and real. I love you with all of my heart.

To Jessica, Joshua, Joel, Asha Joy, and Jonathan, my five incredible kids: You are the light of my life; you keep me humble and always remind me what life is truly about. Words cannot describe how much I love you, and I couldn't be more proud of each of you.

To Rachel Barber, my mom: Thank you for inspiring me with your strength and wisdom, for our talks, and for always making me feel so loved.

To my brothers Tyrone, Greg, and Joseph: Your consistent support over the years has meant so much.

To my friends and neighbors from Wynnefield and Kingsessing in Philly where it all begun, and to my beloved community in Eastlake and south Atlanta where we tested and tried relationships of all sorts: Your imprint on my life will last forever.

To my Mission Year family: There are no words—only incredible memories of how God showed us together that relationships are truly worth it.

To my FCS and CCDA family: We have been able to change the world together. Thanks for loving people and community.

To Helen Lee, my editor, and the IVP team: Your patience has been a great blessing. Thanks for all you have done to make this book possible.

NOTES

p. 25 *There is not a square inch in the whole domain of our human existence*: Abraham Kuyper, The Free University of Amsterdam inaugural address, October 20, 1880. Quoted in *Abraham Kuyper: A Centennial Reader*, ed. James D. Bratt (Grand Rapids: Eerdmans, 1998), 488.

p. 74 *The very first commandment God gave to human beings*: In Genesis 2:15, the Hebrew words *abad* and *shamar* are often translated "cultivate" and "keep"; in other Old Testament passages, though they can be also translated "serve" and "protect," describing a priestly role in regard to sacred space (as with the Levites in the Holy of Holies in Numbers 3:7-8).

p. 122 *#BlackLivesMatter was highlighted at the Urbana 15 Student Missions Conference*: Kevin Porter, "Michelle Higgins Challenges Evangelical Church on #BlackLivesMatter at Urbana 15," December 31, 2015, www.christianpost.com/news/black-lives-matter-ubana-15-michelle-higgins-challenges-evangelical-church-153838.

p. 124 *84 percent of white murder victims are killed by other white people*: "An updated look at statistics on black-on-black murders," Politifact.com, May 21, 2015, www.politifact.com/florida/article/2015/may/21/updated-look-statistics-black-black

-murders. There are some important caveats about these numbers—most importantly is that they don't include every murder. The data only reflects murders that involved a single victim and offender and when the race of the offender was known and reported by police to the FBI.

ABOUT THE AUTHOR

Leroy Barber has dedicated more than twenty-five years to eradicating poverty, confronting homelessness, restoring local neighborhoods, healing racism, and living what Dr. King called "the beloved community." Leroy starts projects that shape society. He is currently the cofounder and director of the Voices Project, college pastor at Kilns College, and director of @HopeMob, and is on the boards of The Simple Way, Missio Alliance, The Evangelical Environmental Network (EEN), and the Christian Community Development Association (CCDA). He is the author of several books, including *Red, Brown, Yellow, Black, White: Who's More Precious in His Sight?* with Velma Maia Thomas and *Everyday Missions: How Ordinary People Can Change the World.*

Leroy has been married to Donna for the past thirty years, and together they have five children.

ABOUT CCDA

C|C CHRISTIAN COMMUNITY
D|A DEVELOPMENT ASSOCIATION

The Christian Community Development Association (CCDA) is a network of Christians committed to engaging with people and communities in the process of transformation. For over twenty-five years, CCDA has aimed to inspire, train, and connect Christians who seek to bear witness to the Kingdom of God by reclaiming and restoring under-resourced communities. CCDA walks alongside local practitioners and partners as they live out Christian Community Development (CCD) by loving their neighbors.

CCDA was founded in 1989 under the leadership of Dr. John Perkins and several other key leaders who are engaged in the work of Christian Community Development still today. Since then, practitioners and partners engaged in the work of the Kingdom have taken ownership of the movement. Our diverse membership and the breadth of the CCDA family are integral to realizing the vision of restored communities.

The CCDA National Conference was birthed as an annual opportunity for practitioners and partners engaged in CCD to gather, sharing best practices, seeking encouragement, inspiration, and connection to other like-minded Christ-followers, committed to ministry in difficult places. For four days, the CCDA family, coming from across the country and around the world, is reunited around a common vision and heart.

Additionally, the CCDA Institute serves as the educational and training arm of the association, offering workshops and trainings in the philosophy of CCD. We have created a space for diverse groups of leaders to be steeped in the heart of CCD and forge lifelong friendships over the course of two years through CCDA's Leadership Cohort.

CCDA has a long-standing commitment to the confrontation of injustice. Our advocacy and organizing is rooted in Jesus' compassion and commitment to Kingdom justice. While we recognize there are many injustices to be fought, as an association we are strategically working on issues of immigration, mass incarceration, and education reform.

To learn more, visit www.ccda.org/ivp

Missio Alliance

Missio Alliance has arisen in response to the shared voice of pastors and ministry leaders from across the landscape of North American Christianity for a new "space" of togetherness and reflection amid the issues and challenges facing the church in our day. We are united by a desire for a fresh expression of evangelical faith, one significantly informed by the global evangelical family. Lausanne's Cape Town Commitment, "A Confession of Faith and a Call to Action," provides an excellent guidepost for our ethos and aims.[1]

Through partnerships with schools, denominational bodies, ministry organizations, and networks of churches and leaders, Missio Alliance addresses the most vital theological and cultural issues facing the North American Church in God's mission today. We do this primarily by convening gatherings, curating resources, and catalyzing innovation in leadership formation.

Rooted in the core convictions of evangelical orthodoxy, the ministry of Missio Alliance is animated by a strong and distinctive theological identity that emphasizes

Comprehensive Mutuality: Advancing the partnered voice and leadership of women and men among the beautiful diversity of the body of Christ across the lines of race, culture and theological heritage.

Hopeful Witness: Advancing a way of being the people of God in the world that reflects an unwavering and joyful hope in the lordship of Christ in the church and over all things.

Church in Mission: Advancing a vision of the local church in which our identity and the power of our testimony is found and expressed though our active participation in God's mission in the world.

In partnership with InterVarsity Press, we are pleased to offer a line of resources authored by a diverse range of theological practitioners. The resources in this series are selected based on the important way in which they address and embody these values, and thus, the unique contribution they offer in equipping Christian leaders for fuller and more faithful participation in God's mission.

[1]www.lausanne.org/content/ctc/ctcommitment